HEINEMANN

SHAKESPEARE

Julius Cæsar

edited by Frank Green

with drama notes and activities by
Rick Lee

Series Editor: John Seely

*In association with the RSA
Shakespeare in Schools Project*

The RSA Shakespeare in Schools Project

The **Heinemann Shakespeare Series** has been developed in association with the **RSA Shakespeare in Schools Project.** Schools in the project have trialled teaching approaches to make Shakespeare accessible to students of all ages and ability levels.

John Seely has worked with schools in the project to develop the unique way of teaching Shakespeare to 11- to 16-year-olds found in **Heinemann Shakespeares.**

The project is a partnership between the RSA (Royal Society for the encouragement of Arts, Manufactures and Commerce), Leicestershire County Council and the Groby family of schools in Leicestershire. It is co-ordinated by the Knighton Fields Advisory Centre for Drama and Dance.

Heinemann Educational
a division of Heinemann Publishers (Oxford) Ltd
Halley Court, Jordan Hill, Oxford OX2 8EJ
OXFORD LONDON EDINBURGH
MADRID ATHENS BOLOGNA PARIS
MELBOURNE SYDNEY AUCKLAND SINGAPORE TOKYO
IBADAN NAIROBI HARARE GABORONE PORTSMOUTH NH (USA)

The text is complete and is based on the Players' Shakespeare

Printed in the *Heinemann Shakespeare Plays* series 1993

94 95 96 97
10 9 8 7 6 5 4 3

A catalogue record for this book is available from the British Library on request.
ISBN 0435 19200 0

Cover design Miller Craig and Cocking
Cover photograph from Donald Cooper
Typeset by Taurus Graphics, Kidlington, Oxon
Printed by Clays Ltd, St Ives plc

Contents

Introduction: *using this book*

This is more than just an edition of *Julius Cæsar* with a few notes. It is a complete guide to studying and enjoying the play.

It begins with an introduction to Shakespeare's theatre, and to the story and characters of the play.

At the end of the book there is guidance on studying the play:
- how to keep tracks of things as you work
- how to take part in a range of drama activities
- understanding Shakespeare's language
- exploring the main theme of government: people and power
- studying the characters
- how to write about the play.

There are also questions and a glossary of specialist words you need when working on the play.

The central part of the book is, of course, the play itself. Here there are several different kinds of help on offer:

Summary: at the top of each double page there is a short summary of what happens on that page.

Grading: alongside the text is a shaded band to help you when working on the play:
1 This is very important text that you probably need to spend extra time on.
2 This is text that you need to read carefully.
3 This is text that you need to spend less time on.
Notes: difficult words, phrases and sentences are explained in simple English

Extra summaries: for the 'white' text the notes are replaced by numbered summaries that give more detail than the ordinary page-by-page summaries.

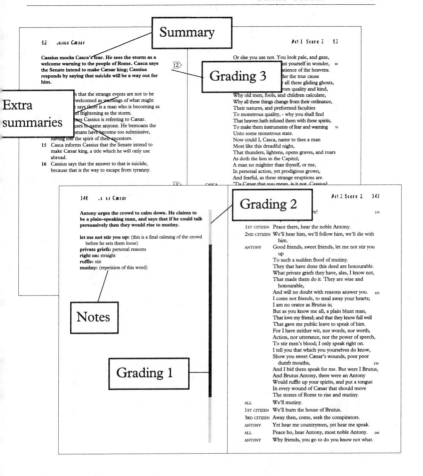

Summary

Grading 3

Extra summaries

Grading 2

Notes

Grading 1

Activities

After every few scenes there is a section containing things to do, helping you focus on the scenes you have just read:

- questions to make sure you have understood the story
- discussion points about the themes and characters of the play
- drama activities
- character work
- close study to help you understand the language of the play
- writing activities.

Shakespeare's theatre

Heavens (A)
the roof above the stage, supported by pillars. Characters could be lowered to the stage during the play

Gallery (B)
used for action on an upper level (or, if not, for the musicians)

Inner space (C)
curtained area that could be opened up to show a new scene

Standing space for audience

Stage (E)
the acting area was very big and had trapdoors so that actors could enter from underneath the stage floor.

Doors (D)
used by the actors, leading from the stage to the tiring house (dressing rooms)

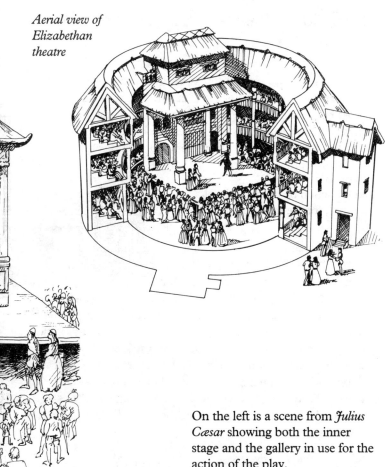

Aerial view of Elizabethan theatre

On the left is a scene from *Julius Cæsar* showing both the inner stage and the gallery in use for the action of the play.

When you have studied the play you should be able to work out exactly which moment in the play this shows. (In Shakespeare's time historical plays were often performed in 'modern dress'.)

Going to the theatre in Shakespeare's day

Theatre going was very popular in Elizabethan London, but it was very different from going to a play today. It was like a cross between going to a football match and going to the theatre. The playhouses were open air and the lack of artificial lighting meant that plays were performed in daylight, normally in the afternoon.

Places were not reserved, so people had to arrive in plenty of time - often more than an hour before the play was due to start. They paid a penny to get into the playhouse, so it was not cheap, since a penny was about one twelfth of a day's wages for a skilled workman. Your penny let you into the large open yard surrounding the stage. The audience here had to stand, looking up at the actors (the stage was 1.5-1.8 metres above the ground). If people wanted a seat, then they had to pay another penny or twopence. This gave admission to the tiers of seating surrounding the yard, and also meant that you had a roof over your head, in case it started to rain. People with even more money could pay to have a seat in an enclosed room. So people of all incomes and social classes attended the theatre and paid for the kind of accommodation they wanted.

While the audience was waiting for the play to begin, people had time to meet friends, talk, eat and drink - in fact they used to continue to enjoy themselves in this way while the play was being performed. But Elizabethan audiences were knowledgeable and enthusiastic. Watching a play was an exciting experience; although the stage was very big, the theatre was quite small, so no one was far from the actors. When an actor had a soliloquy (solo speech) he could come right into the middle of the audience and speak his thoughts in a natural, personal way. At the other extreme the large stage and the three different levels meant that whole battles could be enacted, complete with cannon fire, thunder and lightning and loud military music.

There was no painted stage scenery, so that the audience had to use their imagination to picture the location of each scene, but Shakespeare always gave plenty of word clues in the characters' speeches of when and where a scene takes place. The lack of scenery to move about also meant that scene could follow scene without any break. On the other hand, the theatre companies spared no expense on costumes and furniture and other properties; plays also had live music performed by players placed either in the auditorium close to the stage, or in the gallery above it, if that was not to be used in the play.

Altogether Londoners especially must have considered that going to the theatre was an exciting and important part of their lives; it is believed that up to a fifth of them went to the theatre regularly. Shakespeare and the company in which he became a shareholder, the Lord Chamberlain's Men, worked hard and became wealthy men.

About the Roman Republic

The Roman Empire

Julius Cæsar is set in 44 BC. At that time the Roman Empire had spread far beyond Italy and covered the lands around the Mediterranean Sea, including some of North Africa. To the north the Romans controlled parts of Germany, Belgium and Britain. Therefore, events which took place in Rome had an impact on the whole of that civilised world.

How the Roman Empire was organised

Rome was a republic (a country governed without kings, queens, or emperors). It was governed by the **Senate**, a group of men who met in the Capitol and were called **senators**. When the Senate was first set up the senators were all members of Rome's three most important families, who were looked upon as the 'fathers' of the city. The descendants of these families were known as **Patricians** (in Latin 'pater' means father). The Patricians still formed most of the Senate in 44 BC. By that time, however, the poorer, ordinary people (called the **Plebeians)** were able to elect Tribunes to represent them in the Senate. Even so there was still a great divide between the commoners, and the aristocratic **Patricians**. Some of the Tribunes, elected by the Plebeians, turned against the Plebeians once they were in the Senate.

The Triumvirate

The Senate usually elected two **Consuls** to lead them. However, in 59 BC they had decided on a **Triumvirate**, a leadership of three men. **Julius Cæsar** was one of these three. Julius Cæsar had a reputation as a good soldier and politician, and he returned from the position of Governor of Spain to join Crassus and Pompey as Triumvirs. When Crassus was killed in battle six years later, Cæsar and Pompey began a struggle for overall control. In simple terms, Pompey was in favour of the Republic, or government by the Senate. Pompey accused Cæsar of wanting to take power for himself. Pompey was assassinated by one of his own soldiers in 48 BC and Cæsar was given the title of **Emperor**. Some of Pompey's supporters challenged Cæsar's authority. He fought and beat these supporters in Africa and in Spain. The last of the battles was against Pompey's sons.

The play opens as Cæsar returns in triumph from this victory.

The play

Although *Julius Cæsar* is set in Rome over 2000 years ago it explores themes which are relevant to our own time and which would have been relevant to Elizabethans in Shakespeare's England.

One of the main issues explored in *Julius Cæsar* is the nature of government or people and power. Shakespeare looks at the choices which the Romans had. Four hundred years before the events of the play, the last king of Rome had been removed because he had proved to be like those before him, a dictator who was feared by the people. The monarchy had been replaced by a republic, and the Senate took charge.

At the beginning of *Julius Cæsar*, Cæsar himself has become so powerful that he controls the Senate. It is likely that the Senate will declare him king and he has already named a successor. The Republicans are, of course, appalled. They are former supporters of Pompey who have been accepted by Cæsar, and some of them, notably Brutus, promoted by him.

Cæsar's death is followed by a time of confusion and bloodshed as the Republicans and Cæsar's supporters struggle for power. We might well ask: What is best for the ordinary people? Is there a form of government under which they are better off? The audience of Shakespeare's time would be asking themselves these questions, no doubt, because Queen Elizabeth I was coming to the end of her reign. She had been a very forceful ruler, and had survived plots against her; and there was argument about who her successor would be as she had no children.

Other themes to look out for are: loyalty and friendship; honour; the position of women in Roman society.

Loyalty and friendship We might think that loyalty and friendship are the same thing but Shakespeare shows us it is not always possible to be loyal to our beliefs and our friends.

Honour It was important for true Romans to do things for the right reasons so that they would be respected. They would prefer an honourable death to a dishonourable life.

The role of women The fact that there are only two female characters in the play shows that the society of Rome was a male-dominated one.

The story of the play

The People Celebrate Cæsar's Victories

At the Feast of Lupercal the people of Rome are celebrating another of Cæsar's victories. But not all of the people present are happy at the way things are turning out. Those who have been friends of Pompey fear that Cæsar will take complete control of Rome and the Roman Empire. If that happens, then the Senate - the government - will be powerless and the Republic will be finished. During the celebrations, Antony,

Cæsar's friend, offers Cæsar a mock crown which he refuses, but the Republicans see this as planting the idea of Cæsar becoming king in the minds of the crowd.

Cassius persuades Brutus that Cæar is dangerous

Cassius persuades Brutus that killing Cæsar is the only way to save the Republic. Reluctantly, Brutus agrees, and because he is trusted and respected by everyone he becomes leader of the conspiracy against Cæsar.

The Conspirators kill Cæsar

The next day, the ides of March, the conspirators kill Cæsar on his way to the Senate. Antony is given permission to speak at Cæsar's funeral. Brutus speaks first to justify the murder, and he is so confident of the crowd's support that he leaves when Antony begins to speak. But Brutus underestimates Antony, who convinces the crowd that Cæsar has been their friend and that his assassination must be avenged. The crowd runs riot, and Brutus and Cassius have to flee from Rome.

Antony and Octavius fight Brutus and Cassius

Antony, Octavius and Lepidus form a triumvirate (rule of three) and draw up a list of enemies to be killed. As a result of this, many innocent people die. Antony and Octavius then take their armies East to face Brutus and Cassius, who have managed to form their own armies in the meantime.

The two sides meet at Philippi. Cassius has become superstitious and he has the feeling that he will not survive the battle. Brutus has similar feelings because twice he has been visited by Cæsar's ghost. In the first battle Brutus' army defeat Octavius', but Cassius is beaten by Antony. When Cassius is told that his friend Titinius has been captured he commits suicide. In the second battle Brutus is defeated and kills himself.

The characters of the play

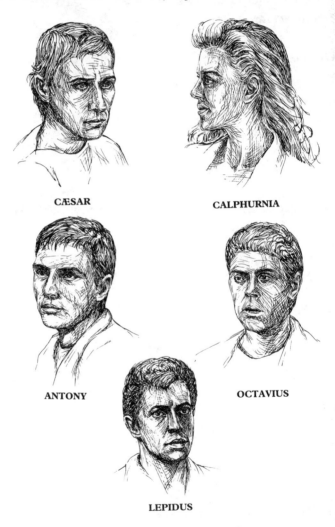

CÆSAR

CALPHURNIA

ANTONY

OCTAVIUS

LEPIDUS

Servants to Antony and Octavius

Cicero
Publius } senators
Popilius Lena

Cinna, a poet

A poet

BRUTUS

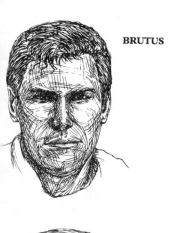

PORTIA

CASSIUS

CASCA

Flavius
Marullus } tribunes

Metellus Cimber
Ligarius
Trebonius } conspirators
Cinna
Decius Brutus

Pindarus, servant to Cassius

Lucius
Dardanius
Strato
Clitus } servants to Brutus
Claudius
Varro

Lucilius
Titinius
Messala } friends of Cassius and Brutus
Cato
Volumnius

Artemidorus, a teacher of rhetoric

Soothsayer
Citizens

Julius Cæsar

Characters

JULIUS CÆSAR

OCTAVIUS CÆSAR

MARK ANTONY

M. ÆMILIUS LEPIDUS

} triumvirs after the death of Julius Cæsar

CICERO

PUBLIUS

POPILIUS LENA

} senators

MARCUS BRUTUS

CASSIUS

CASCA

TREBONIUS

LIGARIUS

DECIUS BRUTUS

METELLUS CIMBER

CINNA

} conspirators against Julius Cæsar

FLAVIUS AND MARULLUS, tribunes

ARTEMIDORUS, a teacher of rhetoric

A SOOTHSAYER

CINNA, a poet

A POET

LUCILIUS, TITINIUS, MESSALA, YOUNG CATO, VOLUMNIUS, friends of Brutus and Cassius

VARRO, CLITUS, CLAUDIUS, STRATO, LUCIUS, DARDANIUS, FLAVIUS, LABEO, servants or officers to Brutus

PINDARUS, servant to Cassius

CALPHURNIA, wife to Cæsar

PORTIA, wife to Brutus

Senators, Citizens, Guards, Attendants, Soldiers

SCENE: *At first Rome, then near Sardis and later near Philippi*

The tribunes, Flavius and Marullus, take the citizens to task for not being at work. A cobbler answers their questions in riddles.

mechanical: workmen
apparel: clothes
cobbler: a play on words: both a maker/repairer of shoes and a clumsy workman.
directly: straight
soles/souls: a play on words: both 'soles' (of shoes) and 'souls'
naughty: worthless
be not out: don't be angry
if you be out: if your shoes are worn out
I can mend you: a play on words. He is saying, 'I can repair your shoes' and, 'I can improve your character'.
awl: tool for piercing leather (Note the play on words: awl/all.)

Act one

Rome: A street
Enter FLAVIUS, MARULLUS, *and certain* CITIZENS
over the stage

FLAVIUS   Hence! home you idle creatures, get you
             home.
             Is this a holiday? What, know you not,
             Being mechanical, you ought not walk
             Upon a labouring day without the sign
             Of your profession? Speak, what trade art thou?

1ST CITIZEN Why sir, a carpenter.

MARULLUS   Where is thy leather apron and thy rule?
             What dost thou with thy best apparel on?
             You sir, what trade are you?

2ND CITIZEN Truly sir, in respect of a fine workman, I am
             but, as you would say, a cobbler.   11

MARULLUS   But what trade art thou? Answer me directly.

2ND CITIZEN A trade sir, that I hope I may use with a safe
             conscience; which is indeed sir, a mender of
             bad soles.

FLAVIUS   What trade thou knave? Thou naughty knave,
             what trade?

2ND CITIZEN Nay I beseech you sir, be not out with me; yet
             if you be out sir, I can mend you.

MARULLUS   What meanest thou by that? Mend me, thou
             saucy fellow?   21

2ND CITIZEN Why sir, cobble you.

FLAVIUS   Thou art a cobbler, art thou?

2ND CITIZEN Truly sir, all that I live by is with the awl: I

The cobbler says that the crowd is out to welcome Caesar back to Rome. Marullus accuses them of forgetting their hero, Pompey.

neat's: cow's
tributaries: captives who must pay money or goods (tributes) to the victor
grace in captive bonds: pay homage by appearing in chains
Tiber: sacred river, running through Rome
replication: echoing
cull: pick
blood: Pompey's sons (blood relatives) defeated by Cæsar

meddle with no tradesman's matters, nor
women's matters, but with all. I am indeed, sir,
a surgeon to old shoes; when they are in great
danger, I recover them. As proper men as ever
trod neat's leather have gone upon my
handiwork.   30

FLAVIUS   But wherefore art not in thy shop today?
               Why dost thou lead these men about the streets?

2ND CITIZEN Truly sir, to wear out their shoes, to get myself
               into more work. But indeed, sir, we make
               holiday to see Cæsar, and to rejoice in his
               triumph.

MARULLUS   Wherefore rejoice? What conquest brings he
                   home?
               What tributaries follow him to Rome,
               To grace in captive bonds his chariot-wheels?
               You blocks, you stones, you worse than
                   senseless things!   40
               O you hard hearts, you cruel men of Rome,
               Knew you not Pompey? Many a time and oft
               Have you climbed up to walls and battlements,
               To towers and windows, yea, to chimney-tops,
               Your infants in your arms, and there have sat
               The livelong day, with patient expectation,
               To see great Pompey pass the streets of Rome.
               And when you saw his chariot but appear,
               Have you not made an universal shout,
               That Tiber trembled underneath her banks,   50
               To hear the replication of your sounds
               Made in her concave shores?
               And do you now put on your best attire?
               And do you now cull out a holiday?
               And do you now strew flowers in his way
               That comes in triumph over Pompey's blood?
               Be gone!
               Run to your houses, fall upon your knees,

Flavius and Marullus leave to clamp down on any celebrations.

intermit: prevent

That needs ... ingratitude: the curse that is bound to fall on the citizens because of this disrespect shown towards Pompey.

weep your tears ... shores of all: fill up the river with your tears

basest mettle: play on words. In Alchemy the basest *metal* was lead, which is soft and can easily be shaped. *Mettle* means a person's spirit, which Flavius also thinks is dull and easily shaped (like lead).

Capitol: the walled area of Rome

disrobe ... ceremonies: take the decorations from any statues

feast of Lupercal: The feast of Lupercal, held on 15th February, was originally a farming festival to discourage wolves from attacking sheep and goats. It became a festival in honour of Pan, the shepherd god of fertility.

the vulgar: common people

These growing feathers ... fearfulness: If we nip this in the bud now it will prevent Cæsar growing so powerful that we shall all have to do as we are told. (This reference to clipping or plucking a bird's wing to limit its flight would be well understood by Elizabethans for whom falconry was a popular sport.)

Pray to the gods to intermit the plague
That needs must light on this ingratitude.   60

FLAVIUS Go, go, good countrymen, and for this fault,
Assemble all the poor men of your sort;
Draw them to Tiber banks, and weep your tears
Into the channel, till the lowest stream
Do kiss the most exalted shores of all.

[Exeunt all the Citizens

See, where their basest mettle be not moved;
They vanish tongue-tied in their guiltiness.
Go you down that way towards the Capitol;
This way will I. Disrobe the images,
If you do find them decked with ceremonies.   70

MARULLUS May we do so?
You know it is the feast of Lupercal.

FLAVIUS It is no matter; let no images
Be hung with Cæsar's trophies. I'll about,
And drive away the vulgar from the streets;
So do you too, where you perceive them thick.
These growing feathers plucked from Cæsar's
    wing
Will make him fly an ordinary pitch,
Who else would soar above the view of men,
And keep us all in servile fearfulness.   80

[Exeunt

Cæsar and his followers appear for the feast of
Lupercal, Antony dressed to take part in the run.
Cæsar urges his childless wife, Calphurnia, to stand
in Antony's way. Cæsar is warned to beware the ides
of March.

When he doth run his course: As part of the celebrations
for the feast of Lupercal, young men ran round the city
boundaries warding off evil spirits with straps of goat
hide. It was said that if women who could not have
children were touched by the straps they would become
fertile.

soothsayer: one who foretells the future

press: crowd

ides of March: 15th March

SCENE **2**

Rome. A street
Flourish. Enter CÆSAR, ANTONY *for the course,*
CALPHURNIA, PORTIA, DECIUS, CICERO, BRUTUS,
CASSIUS, CASCA, *a* SOOTHSAYER, *a great crowd*
following, after them FLAVIUS *and* MARULLUS

CÆSAR	Calphurnia.
CASCA	Peace ho! Cæsar speaks.
CÆSAR	Calphurnia.
CALPHURNIA	Here my lord.
CÆSAR	Stand you directly in Antonius' way,
	When he doth run his course. Antonius.
ANTONY	Cæsar, my lord?
CÆSAR	Forget not, in your speed, Antonius,
	To touch Calphurnia; for our elders say,
	The barren, touched in this holy chase,
	Shake off their sterile curse.
ANTONY	I shall remember. 10
	When Cæsar says, 'Do this', it is performed.
CÆSAR	Set on, and leave no ceremony out.
	[*Music*
SOOTHSAYER	Cæsar!
CÆSAR	Ha! Who calls?
CASCA	Bid every noise be still. Peace yet again!
CÆSAR	Who is it in the press that calls on me?
	I hear a tongue shriller than all the music
	Cry 'Cæsar!' Speak; Cæsar is turned to hear.
SOOTHSAYER	Beward the ides of March.
CÆSAR	What man is that?
BRUTUS	A soothsayer bids you beware the ides of March.
CÆSAR	Set him before me, let me see his face. 20

Cassius accuses Brutus of becoming unfriendly towards him, but Brutus says he merely has something on his mind. Cassius wishes Brutus could see himself as others see him.

order of the course: organised run

gamesome: interested in sports

quick spirit: liveliness

was wont: used

You bear ... loves you: Cassius talks of Brutus' unusual behaviour in terms of horse riding - the hand on the reins is not as sympathetic to the horse as it usually is. (See Metaphor in the Glossary.)

veiled: hidden

countenance: face

passions of some difference: mixed emotions

Conceptions ... myself: thoughts which I cannot share

soil ... behaviours: grounds for my attitude

construe any further: take otherwise

cogitations: thoughts

sees not ... reflection: can only see itself in a reflection

CASSIUS	Fellow, come from the throng, look upon Cæsar.
CÆSAR	What say'st thou to me now? Speak once again.
SOOTHSAYER	Beware the ides of March.
CÆSAR	He is a dreamer, let us leave him. Pass.

[Sennet. Exeunt all except Brutus and Cassius

CASSIUS	Will you go see the order of the course?
BRUTUS	Not I.
CASSIUS	I pray you do.
BRUTUS	I am not gamesome; I do lack some part

Of that quick spirit that is in Antony.
Let me not hinder, Cassius, your desires;
I'll leave you.   31

CASSIUS Brutus, I do observe you now of late;
I have not from your eyes that gentleness
And show of love as I was wont to have.
You bear too stubborn and too strange a hand
Over your friend that loves you.

BRUTUS   Cassius,
Be not deceived. If I have veiled my look,
I turn the trouble of my countenance
Merely upon myself. Vexed I am
Of late with passions of some difference,   40
Conceptions only proper to myself,
Which give some soil perhaps to my behaviours.
But let not therefore my good friends be grieved -
Among which number, Cassius, be you one -
Nor construe any further my neglect,
Than that poor Brutus with himself at war,
Forgets the shows of love to other men.

CASSIUS Then Brutus, I have much mistook your passion;
By means whereof this breast of mine hath buried
Thoughts of great value, worthy cogitations.   50
Tell me good Brutus, can you see your face?

BRUTUS No Cassius; for the eye sees not itself
But by reflection, by some other things.

Cassius says he will help Brutus to see himself as he really is. Brutus asks why Cassius has detained him. Brutus tells Cassius of his fears that Cæsar will be made king.

just: true
shadow: reflection
I have heard ... eyes: Cassius is suggesting to Brutus that many of the most respected citizens in Rome (apart from Cæsar himself), who are suffering badly under Cæsar wish that Brutus would use his eyes (to see what they can see - that Cæsar is ruining them).
seek into ... me: search in my character for qualities I do not possess
jealous: lacking in trust
a common laughter: a joke
did use to stale: made a habit of cheapening
fawn on: wheedle, make up to
after scandal them: immediately afterwards slander them
profess myself ... dangerous: pretend to be friends socially and then become a dangerous enemy
would not: do not want to
impart to: tell
aught toward ... good: anything that is for the good of most people
Set honour ... th'other: Offer me honour and death at the same time

CASSIUS   'Tis just;
And it is very much lamented Brutus,
That you have no such mirrors as will turn
Your hidden worthiness into your eye,
That you might see your shadow. I have heard,
Where many of the best respect in Rome -
Except immortal Cæsar - speaking of Brutus,   60
And groaning underneath this age's yoke,
Have wished that noble Brutus had his eyes.

BRUTUS   Into what dangers would you lead me Cassius,
That you would have me seek into myself
For that which is not in me?

CASSIUS   Therefore good Brutus, be prepared to hear;
And since you know you cannot see yourself
So well as by reflection, I your glass,
Will modestly discover to yourself
That of yourself which you yet know not of.   70
And be not jealous on me, gentle Brutus.
Were I a common laughter, or did use
To stale with ordinary oaths my love
To every new protester; if you know
That I do fawn on men, and hug them hard,
And after scandal them; or if you know
That I profess myself in banqueting
To all the rout, then hold me dangerous.

[Flourish, and shout.

BRUTUS   What means this shouting? I do fear the people
Choose Cæsar for their king.

CASSIUS   Ay, do you fear it? 80
Then must I think you would not have it so.

BRUTUS   I would not Cassius, yet I love him well.
But wherefore do you hold me here so long?
What is it that you would impart to me?
If it be aught toward the general good,
Set honour in one eye and death i' th' other,

Cassius recalls Cæsar floundering in the Tiber and later being struck down by fever in Spain.

indifferently: impartially
speed me: give me prosperity
favour: appearance
had as lief: would rather
such a … myself: somebody who is no different from me
chafing with: angrily beating
Accoutred: dressed
buffet: beat
lusty: strong, vigorous
stemming it … controversy: stopping it by the strength with which we opposed it
the point proposed: the place we were aiming for
Aeneas: a Trojan prince who, when the Greeks burned Troy escaped with his father Anchises and his son Ascanius, and settled in Italy with his family. Romans believed that he was the ancestor of the Roman Emperors.
did from … fly: lost their colour

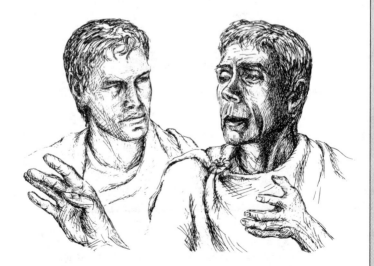

And I will look on both indifferently;
For let the gods so speed me as I love
The name of honour more than I fear death.

CASSIUS   I know that virtue to be in you Brutus,   90
As well as I do know your outward favour.
Well, honour is the subject of my story.
I cannot tell what you and other men
Think of this life; but for my single self,
I had as lief not be, as live to be
In awe of such a thing as I myself.
I was born free as Cæsar, so were you;
We both have fed as well, and we can both
Endure the winter's cold as well as he.
For once, upon a raw and gusty day,   100
The troubled Tiber chafing with her shores,
Cæsar said to me, 'Darest thou Cassius now
Leap in with me into this angry flood,
And swim to yonder point?' Upon the word,
Accoutred as I was, I plunged in,
And bade him follow; so indeed he did.
The torrent roared, and we did buffet it
With lusty sinews, throwing it aside,
And stemming it with hearts of controversy.
But ere we could arrive the point proposed,   110
Cæsar cried, 'Help me Cassius, or I sink.'
I, as Æneas, our great ancestor,
Did from the flames of Troy upon his shoulder
The old Anchises bear, so from the waves of
     Tiber
Did I the tired Cæsar. And this man
Is now become a god, and Cassius is
A wretched creature, and must bend his body,
If Cæsar carelessly but nod on him.
He had a fever when he was in Spain,
And when the fit was on him, I did mark   120
How he did shake. 'Tis true, this god did shake;
His coward lips did from their colour fly,

Cassius is amazed that someone so weak should be regarded so highly. Brutus fears Cæsar has been awarded more honours. Cassius urges Brutus to consider himself Cæsar's equal.

bend: look
lustre: brightness
get the start of: overtake, lead
palm: palm leaf, sign of victory
Colossus: one of the seven wonders of the ancient world, Colossus was a huge statue, the feet of which were set on either side of the entrance to Rhodes harbour.
petty: insignificant
Men ... fates: there are times when man has the opportunity to decide his own future
underlings: inferiors
conjure: call up spirits.
Age, thou art shamed: this generation is in disgrace
When went there by: when has there been
the great flood: In classical mythology Zeus wanted to destroy the whole world because men were so sinful.
But it was ... man: that had only one famous man by which it was remembered

And that same eye whose bend doth awe the
    world
Did lose his lustre; I did hear him groan;
Ay, and that tongue of his, that bade the Romans
Mark him and write his speeches in their books,
Alas, it cried, 'Give me some drink Titinius,'
As a sick girl. Ye gods, it doth amaze me
A man of such a feeble temper should
So get the start of the majestic world,
And bear the palm alone.   131

[Shout. Flourish

BRUTUS   Another general shout?
I do believe that these applauses are
For some new honours that are heaped on Cæsar.

CASSIUS   Why man, he doth bestride the narrow world
Like a Colossus, and we petty men
Walk under his huge legs, and peep about
To find ourselves dishonourable graves.
Men at some time are masters of their fates:
The fault, dear Brutus, is not in our stars,   140
But in ourselves, that we are underlings.
Brutus and Cæsar. What should be in that
    'Cæsar'?
Why should that name be sounded more than
    yours?
Write them together, yours is as fair a name;
Sound them, it doth become the mouth as well;
Weigh them, it is as heavy; conjure with 'em,
Brutus will start a spirit as soon as Cæsar.
Now in the names of all the gods at once,
Upon what meat doth this our Cæsar feed,
That he is grown so great? Age, thou art shamed. 150
Rome, thou hast lost the breed of noble bloods.
When went there by an age since the great flood,
But it was famed with more than with one man?

Cassius reminds Brutus of his ancestor's treatment of royalty. Brutus promises to think over what has been said. Cæsar and his party return from the Lupercalia.

encompassed: contained

Rome/room: (Play on Words, see Glossary)

There was a Brutus once: Approximately 400 years previously Lucius Junius Brutus, probably an ancestor of this Brutus, established the Republic in Rome after expelling the tyrannical Tarquin royal family.

would have brooked ... as a king: would have put up with the devil in Rome as willingly as he would tolerate a king.

I am nothing jealous: I don't doubt

have some aim: can guess

recount hereafter: tell you later

For this ... moved: For now I ask you out of kindness not to try to persuade me any more.

Brutus ... upon us: I will take no pride in being a Roman if what is likely to happen takes place

Both meet: suitable both to

after his sour fashion: in his usual sour way

chidden: told off/rebuked

	When could they say, till now, that talked of Rome,
	That her wide walks encompassed but one man?
	Now is it Rome indeed, and room enough,
	When there is in it but one only man.
	O you and I have heard our fathers say,
	There was a Brutus once that would have brooked
	Th' eternal devil to keep his state in Rome 160
	As easily as a king.
BRUTUS	That you do love me, I am nothing jealous;
	What you would work me to, I have some aim:
	How I have thought of this, and of these times,
	I shall recount hereafter. For this present,
	I would not, so with love I might entreat you,
	Be any further moved. What you have said,
	I will consider; what you have to say,
	I will with patience hear, and find a time
	Both meet to hear and answer such high things. 170
	Till then, my noble friend, chew upon this:
	Brutus had rather be a villager
	Than to repute himself a son of Rome
	Under these hard conditions as this time
	Is like to lay upon us.
CASSIUS	I am glad
	That my weak words have struck but thus much show
	Of fire from Brutus.
BRUTUS	The games are done, and Cæsar is returning.
CASSIUS	As they pass by, pluck Casca by the sleeve,
	And he will, after his sour fashion, tell you 180
	What hath proceeded worthy note today.

Enter CÆSAR *and his Train*

BRUTUS	I will do so. But look you Cassius,
	The angry spot doth glow on Cæsar's brow,
	And all the rest look like a chidden train;

Cæsar tells Antony that if he were a man who knew fear, then Cassius would frighten him for he is not to be trusted. He asks for Antony's views. Brutus and Cassius begin questioning Casca.

Sleek-headed: smooth haired
well given: friendly
would: I wish
spare: thin
Yet if my … fear: if being afraid was part of my personality
looks … men: understands men's motives
Such men … themselves: men like him are never happy while they know there is someone around who is more powerful than they are
I rather … Cæsar: I'm telling you what there is to be afraid of, not what I am afraid of (because I am Cæsar).
chanced: happened

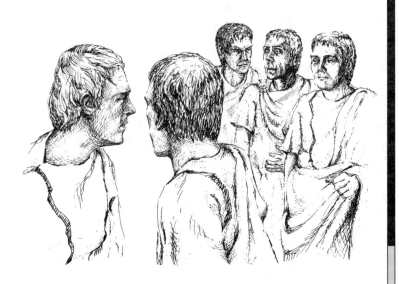

	Calphurnia's cheek is pale, and Cicero	
	Looks with such ferret and such fiery eyes	
	As we have seen him in the Capitol,	
	Being crossed in conference by some senators.	
CASSIUS	Casca will tell us what the matter is.	
CÆSAR	Antonius.	190
ANTONY	Cæsar?	
CÆSAR	Let me have men about me that are fat,	
	Sleek-headed men, and such as sleep a-nights.	
	Yond Cassius has a lean and hungry look;	
	He thinks too much. Such men are dangerous.	
ANTONY	Fear him not Cæsar, he's not dangerous.	
	He is a noble Roman, and well given.	
CÆSAR	Would he were fatter. But I fear him not.	
	Yet if my name were liable to fear,	
	I do not know the man I should avoid	200
	So soon as that spare Cassius. He reads much,	
	He is a great observer, and he looks	
	Quite through the deeds of men. He loves no plays,	
	As thou dost Antony; he hears no music;	
	Seldom he smiles, and smiles in such a sort	
	As if he mocked himself, and scorned his spirit	
	That could be moved to smile at any thing.	
	Such men as he be never at heart's ease	
	While they behold a greater than themselves,	
	And therefore are they very dangerous.	210
	I rather tell thee what is to be feared	
	That what I fear; for always I am Cæsar.	
	Come on my right hand, for this ear is deaf,	
	And tell me truly what thou think'st of him.	

[Sennet. Exeunt Cæsar and his Train

| CASCA | You pulled me by the cloak; would you speak with me? |
| BRUTUS | Ay Casca, tell us what hath chanced today |

Casca tells Brutus and Cassius that Cæsar refused the offer of a crown three times. When the crowd showed their approval of this, Cæsar fell down in a faint.

thrice: three times
marry: by the Virgin Mary
marry was't: I'll say it was
gentle: Brutus is aware that Casca is losing patience with their questions.

1 Casca did not pay close attention because he took it as a joke, since the crown which Antony offered Cæsar was not a proper crown at all. Cæsar refused the crown three times; each time more unwillingly, it seemed to Casca. After the third time, the crowd roared so loudly in approval that Cæsar fell in a faint. Casca was amused by this but dared not laugh for fear of inhaling the smell of the crowd.

1

	That Cæsar looks so sad.
CASCA	Why you were with him, were you not?
BRUTUS	I should not then ask Casca what had chanced. 220
CASCA	Why there was a crown offered him; and being offered him, he put it by with the back of his hand, thus; and the people fell a-shouting.
BRUTUS	What was the second noise for?
CASCA	Why for that too.
CASSIUS	They shouted thrice. What was the last cry for?
CASCA	Why for that too.
BRUTUS	Was the crown offered him thrice?
CASCA	Ay marry was't, and he put it by thrice, every time gentler than other; and at every putting-by mine honest neighbours shouted. 231
CASSIUS	Who offered him the crown?
CASCA	Why Antony.
BRUTUS	Tell us the manner of it, gentle Casca.

CASCA   I can as well be hanged as tell the manner of it. It was mere foolery; I did not mark it. I saw Mark Antony offer him a crown, yet 'twas not a crown neither, 'twas one of these coronets; and as I told you, he put it by once: but for all that, to my thinking, he would fain have had it. Then he offered it to him again; then he put it by again; but to my thinking, he was very loath to lay his fingers off it. And then he offered it the third time; he put it the third time by; and still as he refused it, the rabblement hooted, and clapped their chopped hands, and threw up their sweaty night-caps, and uttered such a deal of stinking breath because Cæsar refused the crown, that it had almost choked Cæsar; for he swounded, and fell down at it. And for mine own part, I durst not laugh, for fear of opening my lips and receiving the bad air.   252

Before Cæsar fell he had offered the crowd his throat to cut. When he recovered he left.

2 Cassius wants confirmation that Cæsar fainted.

3 Casca explains how Cæsar foamed at the mouth, unable to speak.

4 Brutus sees this as Cæsar's illness to which Cassius referred earlier, the falling sickness or epilepsy.

5 Cassius interprets 'falling sickness' as giving way to a tyrant. (see Play on Words in the Glossary)

6 Casca says the crowd behaved as if they were in a theatre and Cæsar was performing on stage. When he saw how pleased the crowd was that he had refused the crown, Cæsar bared his throat for the crowd to cut. Casca says that if he had been in the crowd he would have taken up the offer. Cæsar then fell. When he recovered he begged for forgiveness, and this the crowd gave him, willingly.

7 At that point Cæsar left the celebrations.

8 Cassius asks if Cicero, a famous Roman orator (whose writings about the classical world were well known and respected in Shakespeare's time), had anything to say.

9 Casca says that Cicero did speak, but in Greek, and so he cannot tell them what was said.

CASSIUS   But soft I pray you; what, did Cæsar swound?

CASCA   He fell down in the market-place, and foamed at
          mouth, and was speechless.

BRUTUS   'Tis very like he hath the falling sickness.

CASSIUS   No, Cæsar hath it not; but you, and I,
          And honest Casca, we have the falling sickness.

CASCA   I know not what you mean by that, but I am sure
          Cæsar fell down. If the tag-rag people did not clap
          him and hiss him, according as he pleased and
          displeased them, as they use to do the players in the
          theatre, I am no true man.   263

BRUTUS   What said he when he came unto himself?

CASCA   Marry, before he fell down, when he perceived the
          common herd was glad he refused the crown, he
          plucked me ope his doublet, and offered them his
          throat to cut. An I had been a man of any occupa-
          tion, if I would not have taken him at a word, I
          would I might go to hell among the rogues. And so
          he fell. When he came to himself again, he said, if he
          had done or said anything amiss, he desired their
          worships to think it was his infirmity. Three or four
          wenches where I stood cried, 'Alas good soul,' and
          forgave him with all their hearts. But there's no heed
          to be taken of them; if Cæsar had stabbed their
          mothers, they would have done no less.

BRUTUS   And after that, he came thus sad away?

CASCA   Ay.

CASSIUS   Did Cicero say any thing?   280

CASCA   Ay, he spoke Greek.

CASSIUS   To what effect?

CASCA   Nay, an I tell you that, I'll ne'er look you i' th'
          face again. But those that understood him smiled
          at one another, and shook their heads; but for
          mine own part, it was Greek to me. I could tell
          you more news too: Marullus and Flavius, for

Flavius and Marullus have been executed. After Casca has left, Brutus and Cassius discuss him. They arrange to meet the following day. Cassius has a plan to convince Brutus of his popularity.

10
11
12

10 Casca has news that Flavius and Marullus have been executed for taking decorations from Cæsar's statues. Other things happened, but too trivial to remember.

11 Cassius invites Casca to supper, but he has a previous engagement. Casca accepts an invitation for the following day, if the food is good!

12 Casca leaves

blunt: dull

quick mettle: intelligent

tardy form: slow appearance

This rudeness ... better appetite: this outspokenness makes people better prepared to listen to him.

think of the world: give some thought to our situation

Thy honourable mettle ... disposed: your noble personality can be persuaded into an unusual course of action (again, metal/mettle; wrought iron is shaped metal)

Therefore it is meet ... seduced: So it is much better if men with noble minds keep the company of other similar men - for who has such a strong character that he cannot be led astray?

bear me hard: treat me harshly

If I were ... me: If I were Brutus and Brutus were Cassius I would not listen to him. (Although Cassius is about the same age as Cæsar, in his early fifties, and Brutus is ten years younger, Cæsar has favoured Brutus whilst ignoring Cassius.)

several hands: different styles of handwriting

pulling scarfs off Cæsar's images, are put to
silence. Fare you well. There was more foolery
yet, if I could remember it.   290

CASSIUS   Will you sup with me tonight, Casca?

CASCA   No, I am promised forth.

CASSIUS   Will you dine with me tomorrow?

CASCA   Ay, if I be alive, and your mind hold, and your
dinner worth the eating.

CASSIUS   Good; I will expect you.

CASCA   Do so. Farewell both.

[*Exit*

BRUTUS   What a blunt fellow is this grown to be!
He was quick mettle when he went to school.

CASSIUS   So is he now in execution.   300
Of any bold or noble enterprise,
However he puts on this tardy form.
This rudeness is a sauce to his good wit,
Which gives men stomach to digest his words
With better appetite.

BRUTUS   And so it is. For this time I will leave you.
Tomorrow, if you please to speak with me,
I will come home to you; or, if you will,
Come home to me, and I will wait for you.

CASSIUS   I will do so. Till then, think of the world.   310

[*Exit Brutus*

Well Brutus, thou art noble; yet I see
Thy honourable mettle may be wrought
From that it is disposed. Therefore it is meet
That noble minds keep ever with their likes;
For who so firm that cannot be seduced?
Cæsar doth bear me hard, but he loves Brutus.
If I were Brutus now, and he were Cassius,
He should not humour me. I will this night,
In several hands, in at his windows throw,

obscurely ... at: hinting at Caesar's intentions

Keeping track

Scene 1

1 Flavius and Marullus are tribunes, elected to represent the ordinary people. Knowing this, is there anything in their attitude which strikes you as odd?

Scene 2

2 What has been the relationship between Brutus and Cassius?

3 How has Cassius aroused Brutus' suspicions in line 63?

4 Brutus responds to the noise of the crowd, but Cassius seems to ignore this and immediately launches into another attack on Cæsar. Why is this?

5 Marullus and Flavius are executed. What does this tell us about Cæsar?

6 What is the difference in the ways that Brutus and Cassius see Casca?

As if they came from several citizens,   320
Writings, all tending to the great opinion
That Rome holds of his name; wherein obscurely
Cæsar's ambition shall be glanced at.
And after this let Cæsar seat him sure,
For we will shake him, or worse days endure.

[*Exit*

Discussion

1 Were Flavius and Marullus honourable and
   courageous, or naive and stupid?
2 The ides of a month (15th of some months,13th of
   others) were considered an unlucky time. The Romans
   were superstitious people - as were the Elizabethans
   who would understand the importance of the
   prediction. What thoughts might be going through
   Cæsar's mind in Act 1 scene 2 lines 18-23?

Drama

'*Such men are dangerous*'.

Groups of four.
Cæsar is a suspicious man (see lines 192 - 193 'Let me
have men') and almost certainly has spies.

1 You are those spies and were in the crowd taking
   photographs secretly. Create the photographs (see
   p243) which would best demonstrate that Brutus,
   Cassius and Casca are dangerous men – probably
   conspirators.
2 You were also able to overhear their conversations.

Select two or three lines each which would support the conspiracy theory. Repeat them and record them on tape. Make sure you get evidence against all three men.

3 Present your findings to Cæsar (your teacher).

A statue of Cæsar

Groups of five.

Marullus and Flavius are put to death for removing scarves from Cæsar's statues. It is likely that Cæsar would be having statues made of himself. Imagine you are a team of stone-masons who have been asked to make statues of Cæsar to be placed in the streets.

Choose from the following titles:

Cæsar - Man of the People

Cæsar - The Conqueror

Cæsar - The Bravest Roman

Cæsar - The Lion

What other titles might you choose? Make a statue and when you are satisfied with it, each group could show theirs to Cæsar (your teacher) to see who is going to get paid! (see page 243 for help on **Statues**)

Character

Very briefly, how do the following feel about Cæsar?

1 Brutus

2 Cassius

3 Casca

Close study

1 Look at lines 32-161. How does Cassius persuade Brutus to give him his attention and then begin to see things his way?

2 Look at Casca's version of the events of the feast of Lupercal in Scene 2, particularly lines 239-40, 242-243 and 250-252. Does this reveal why Cassius especially chose Casca to tell them what happened?

Writing

You are a reporter from a Roman newspaper, attending the feast of Lupercal. Your story is front page news. Write your report with a headline, subheadings if necessary, and a 'photograph' if you think it suitable.

Quiz

Who said the following, and to whom?
1 'You blocks, you stones, you worse than senseless things'
2 'Beware the ides of March'
3 'I have not from your eyes that gentleness
And show of love as I was wont to have.'

Who said the following and about whom?
4 'He doth bestride the narrow world
Like a Colossus'
5 'He thinks too much: such men are dangerous'
6 'What a blunt fellow he is grown to be.'

Do you remember...
7 Who was called 'naughty knave' and 'saucy fellow'?
8 Why Calphurnia was told to stand in Antony's way?
9 Who claimed to have saved Cæsar from drowning?
10 Why Flavius and Marullus were executed?

It is the night of the feast of Lupercal, the night before the ides of March. Casca interprets strange events as bad omens.

1 Cicero asks Casca if he has accompanied Cæsar home, and comments on Casca's frightened look.

2 Casca says he has seen storms before, but nothing like this. He believes the gods are fighting amongst themselves, or showing their displeasure at man's behaviour.

3 Cicero suggests that nature is to be admired.

4 Casca gives examples of unnatural events: a slave with his hand on fire, feeling no pain; an escaped lion not taking advantage of its freedom; men in flames, walking about the streets; and, the previous day, an owl hooting in the market-place at midday. He tells Cicero that such happenings cannot be explained away with reasoned argument.

1 >
2 >

3 >
4 >

SCENE **3**

Rome. A street.
Thunder and lightning. Enter CASCA *and* CICERO

CICERO   Good even, Casca: brought you Cæsar home?
      Why are you breathless, and why stare you so?

CASCA   Are not you moved, when all the sway of earth
      Shakes like a thing unfirm? O Cicero,
      I have seen tempests, when the scolding winds
      Have rived the knotty oaks, and I have seen
      Th' ambitious ocean swell, and rage, and foam,
      To be exalted with the threat'ning clouds;
      But never till tonight, never till now,
      Did I go through a tempest dropping fire.   10
      Either there is a civil strife in heaven,
      Or else the world, too saucy with the gods,
      Incenses them to send destruction.

CICERO   Why, saw you any thing more wonderful?

CASCA   A common slave - you know him well by sight -
      Held up his left hand, which did flame and burn
      Like twenty torches joined; and yet his hand,
      Not sensible of fire, remained unscorched.
      Besides - I ha' not since put up my sword -
      Against the Capitol I met a lion,   20
      Who glazed upon me, and went surly by,
      Without annoying me. And there were drawn
      Upon a heap, a hundred ghastly women,
      Transformed with their fear, who swore they saw
      Men, all in fire, walk up and down the streets.
      And yesterday the bird of night did sit,
      Even at noon-day, upon the market-place,
      Hooting and shrieking. When these prodigies
      Do so conjointly meet, let not men say,
      'These are their reasons - they are natural'.   30

Cicero warns against misinterpretation. Cassius enters. To Casca's horror, Cassius has been challenging the elements to do their worst.

5 >

6 >

5 Casca believes the omens are bad.

6 Cicero agrees that strange events are taking place, but warns Casca against reading too much into them.

7 >

7 Casca confirms that Cæsar intends to be at the Capitol next day.

8 Cicero leaves.

9 Cassius enters and knows Casca by his voice. Cassius has bared his chest to the storm, having no fear.

8 >

10 Casca is horrified that Cassius has so tempted fate. He says men should tremble when the gods behave in this way.

9 >

11 Cassius accuses Casca of being unimaginative.

10 >

11 >

	For I believe, they are portentous things
	Unto the climate that they point upon.
CICERO	Indeed, it is a strange-disposed time.
	But men may construe things after their fashion.
	Clean from the purpose of the things themselves.
	Comes Cæsar to the Capitol tomorrow?
CASCA	He doth; for he did bid Antonius
	Send word to you he would be there tomorrow.
CICERO	Good night then, Casca; this disturbed sky
	Is not to walk in.
CASCA	Farewell Cicero. 40

[Exit Cicero

Enter CASSIUS

CASSIUS	Who's there?
CASCA	A Roman.
CASSIUS	Casca, by your voice.
CASCA	Your ear is good. Cassius, what a night is this!
CASSIUS	A very pleasing night to honest men.
CASCA	Who ever knew the heavens menace so?
CASSIUS	Those that have known the earth so full of faults.
	For my part, I have walked about the streets,
	Submitting me unto the perilous night;
	And thus unbraced, Casca, as you see,
	Have bared my bosom to the thunderstone;
	And when the cross blue lightning seemed to open 50
	The breast of heaven, I did present myself
	Even in the aim and very flash of it.
CASCA	But wherefore did you so much tempt the heavens?
	It is the part of men to fear and tremble,
	When the most mighty gods by tokens send
	Such dreadful heralds to astonish us.
CASSIUS	You are dull, Casca, and those sparks of life
	That should be in a Roman you do want,

Cassius mocks Casca's fear. He sees the storm as a welcome warning to the people of Rome. Casca says the Senate intend to make Cæsar king; Cassius responds by saying that suicide will be a way out for him.

12〉

12 Cassius says that the strange events are not to be feared, but welcomed as warnings of what might happen. He says there is a man who is becoming as powerful and frightening as the storm.

13 Casca assumes Cassius is referring to Cæsar.

14 Cassius refuses to name anyone. He bemoans the fact that Romans have become too submissive, having lost the spirit of their ancestors.

15 Casca informs Cassius that the Senate intend to make Cæsar king, a title which he will only use abroad.

16 Cassius says that the answer to that is suicide, because that is the way to escape from tyranny.

13〉
14〉

15〉

16〉

Or else you use not. You look pale, and gaze,
And put on fear, and cast yourself in wonder, 60
To see the strange impatience of the heavens.
But if you would consider the true cause
Why all these fires, why all these gliding ghosts,
Why birds and beasts from quality and kind,
Why old men, fools, and children calculate,
Why all these things change from their ordinance,
Their natures, and preformed faculties
To monstrous quality, - why you shall find
That heaven hath infused them with these spirits,
To make them instruments of fear and warning 70
Unto some monstrous state.
Now could I, Casca, name to thee a man
Most like this dreadful night,
That thunders, lightens, opens graves, and roars
As doth the lion in the Capitol;
A man no mightier than thyself, or me,
In personal action, yet prodigious grown,
And fearful, as these strange eruptions are.

CASCA   'Tis Cæsar that you mean, is it not, Cassius?

CASSIUS   Let it be who it is; for Romans now 80
Have thews and limbs like to their ancestors;
But, woe the while, our fathers' minds are dead,
And we are governed with our mothers' spirits:
Our yoke and sufferance show us womanish.

CASCA   Indeed, they say the senators tomorrow
Mean to establish Cæsar as a king;
And he shall wear his crown by sea and land,
In every place, save here in Italy.

CASSIUS   I know where I will wear this dagger then;
Cassius from bondage will deliver Cassius. 90
Therein, ye gods, you make the weak most strong;
Therein, ye gods, you tyrants do defeat.
Nor stony tower, nor walls of beaten brass,
Nor airless dungeon, nor strong links of iron,
Can be retentive to the strength of spirit;

Casca agrees with Cassius' condemnation of Cæsar, and declares he will do as much as anyone to put things right. Cassius informs him that he has organised a conspiracy.

17 Casca says that every man has it within his power to be free.

18 Cassius is certain that Cæsar could not be so powerful if Romans stood up to him; but they are weak and serve only as a means of making Cæsar strong. Cassius wonders if he has said too much to Casca.

19 Casca assures Cassius that he is to be trusted. He says that if there is a faction (group) willing to act against Cæsar, then he wants to be included.

20 Cassius welcomes Casca's commitment, and tells him that others are already recruited. They are all to meet later by the marble columns outside Pompey's theatre. He says the night is suited to their purpose, because honest people will stay at home, and the weather is as evil as the plan they have in mind.

17

18

19

20

But life, being weary of these worldly bars,
Never lacks power to dismiss itself.
If I know this, know all the world besides,
That part of tyranny that I do bear
I can shake off at pleasure.

[*Thunder still*

CASCA   So can I.   100
So every bondman in his own hand bears
The power to cancel his captivity.

CASSIUS And why should Cæsar be a tyrant then?
Poor man, I know he would not be a wolf,
But that he sees the Romans are but sheep;
He were no lion, were not Romans hinds.
Those that with haste will make a mighty fire
Begin it with weak straws. What trash is Rome,
What rubbish, and what offal, when it serves
For the base matter to illuminate   110
So vile a thing as Cæsar! But, O grief,
Where hast thou led me? I perhaps speak this
Before a willing bondman; then I know
My answer must be made. But I am armed,
And dangers are to me indifferent.

CASCA You speak to Casca, and to such a man
That is no fleering tell-tale. Hold, my hand.
Be factious for redress of all these griefs,
And I will set this foot of mine as far
As who goes farthest.

CASSIUS   There's a bargain made.   120
Now know you, Casca, I have moved already
Some certain of the noblest-minded Romans
To undergo with me an enterprise
Of honourable-dangerous consequence;
And I do know, by this, they stay for me
In Pompey's porch; for now, this fearful night,
There is no stir or walking in the streets;
And the complexion of the element

**Cinna enters and suggests that Brutus would give
credibility to the conspiracy. Cassius gives him letters
to deliver for Brutus to find.**

21 Cassius recognises Cinna by his walk. He asks him why
   he is in such a hurry. Cinna is looking for Cassius.

22 Cassius introduces Casca as a fellow-conspirator. He
   asks if the others are waiting for him.

23 Cinna is pleased to welcome Casca to their number.

24 Cassius again asks if the others are waiting for him.

25 Cinna confirms that they are. He would like to see
   Brutus join them, too.

26 Cassius assures him that he has that in hand. He
   gives Cinna some letters and asks him to leave them
   in places where Brutus will be sure to find them.
   Cassius then tells him that they will all meet later.
   For the third time he asks if the others are waiting;
   he asks particularly about Decius Brutus and
   Trebonius.

27 Cinna says Metellus Cimber is looking for Cassius.
   The others are waiting.

28 Cassius assures Casca that Brutus is on the verge of
   joining them.

21
22
23
24
25
26
27
28

In favour's like the work we have in hand,
Most bloody, fiery, and most terrible.   130

Enter CINNA

CASCA	Stand close awhile, for here comes one in haste.
CASSIUS	'Tis Cinna; I do know him by his gait;
	He is a friend. Cinna, where haste you so?
CINNA	To find out you. Who's that? Metellus Cimber?
CASSIUS	No, it is Casca, one incorporate
	To our attempts. Am I not stayed for, Cinna?
CINNA	I am glad on't. What a fearful night is this!
	There's two or three of us have seen strange
	sights.
CASSIUS	Am I not stayed for? Tell me.
CINNA	Yes, you are. 140
	O Cassius, if you could
	But win the noble Brutus to our party -
CASSIUS	Be you content. Good Cinna, take this paper,
	And look you lay it in the prætor's chair,
	Where Brutus may but find it. And throw this
	In at his window. Set this up with wax
	Upon old Brutus' statue. All this done,
	Repair to Pompey's porch, where you shall find us.
	Is Decius Brutus and Trebonius there?
CINNA	All but Metellus Cimber, and he's gone
	To seek you at your house. Well, I will hie, 150
	And so bestow these papers as you bade me.
CASSIUS	That done, repair to Pompey's theatre.

[*Exit* CINNA

Come Casca, you and I will yet ere day
See Brutus at his house. Three parts of him
Is ours already, and the man entire
Upon the next encounter yields him ours.

| CASCA | O he sits high in all the people's hearts; |

Casca and Cassius discuss Brutus' qualities

29 >

29 Casca appreciates that Brutus' support for the conspiracy would make it acceptable to the people of Rome.

30 >

30 Cassius agrees and says that Brutus will be among their number before dawn.

ACTIVITIES

Keeping track

1 What are the main differences between Casca and Cicero?

2 The next day is the ides of March. Why is it important that the audience is reminded that Cæsar intends to be at the Capitol?

3 When does Cassius first make absolutely clear to Casca his feelings about Cæsar?

4 Cassius is concerned that those in the conspiracy should be waiting for him. What would it have meant had they not been there?

5 Why are the conspirators so keen for Brutus to join them?

Discussion

1 How can the storm best be presented on stage? What would be the details of the special effects (i.e. how would you produce thunder, lightning, the effect of rain?)? Would the effects be haphazard or scripted to occur in appropriate places? Work out a 'special

And that which would appear offence in us,
His countenance, like richest alchemy,
Will change to virtue and to worthiness.   160

CASSIUS   Him and his worth, and our great need of him
You have right well conceited. Let us go,
For it is after midnight; and ere day
We will awake him, and be sure of him.

[*Exeunt*

effects' script for lines 1–40.

2 Cassius has gathered a group of conspirators. What sort
of people would he have approached? What might he
have said? Would he approach them as a group, or
individually?

3 Cæsar's victory in Spain (October 45 BC) is celebrated on
the feast of Lupercal (15th February, 44 BC) which is the
day before the ides of March (15th March, 44 BC). The
dates in brackets are actual time, as opposed to
Shakespeare-time. Can you suggest why Shakespeare has
compressed time in this way? What does he achieve?

Close study

The use of prose and blank verse in Act 1 scene 1 is
straightforward in that the ordinary people speak in prose, the
others in verse. (See **Shakespeare's Language,** page 238).
Can you explain, however, why Casca might use prose in
Act 1 scene 2 and blank verse in Act 1 scene 3? Think about
these points:

- The discussion between Brutus and Cassius at the end of Act 1 scene 2. (This should help with his use of prose.)
- His state of mind in Act 1 scene 3. (This should help with his use of verse.)

Drama

Bloody, fiery and most terrible

In this scene Cassius seems to be at one with the storm, buffeting Casca into conspiracy. With his shirt undone and yelling with the storm, he must seem mad to Casca. This is meant to be melodramatic and frightening. See if you can create this atmosphere with your voices.

Whole class activity.
1 Divide between you lines 41 ('Who's there...') to 130 ('most terrible...').
2 Each person should have about three lines, but divide the speech into sections that make sense (so look at the punctuation).

Groups of 4, 5, or 6.
3 The class now divides so that the whole extract can be practised in sections (so speakers A, B, C, D, and E work together, and so on.)
4 Practise your lines together. This will work best if you learn them.
5 Try to get Cassius' storm-driven anger and Casca's fearfulness into your voices. Find those sounds that are like the sound of the wind, thunder and lightning - only use your voices.
6 As well as practising the words, you could use storm noise effects (see Discussion, question 1) which you could produce when it is not your turn to speak.

Whole class activity.

7 When all the small groups have practised, the whole class then brings all the lines together.

8 Now add the storm backing noises while the lines are spoken. (You could make this easier by first recording the storm noises on tape and have this as a backing for your spoken lines. Then you can record the whole thing.)

Character

Match the following qualities with the appropriate characters on the next page:

Qualities

A hated
  self-important
  ambitious
  claims to be brave
  powerful
  physically weak

C thoughtful
  respected
  honourable
  troubled
  shrewd
  proud

B appears unintelligent...
  ...but is alert
  reliable
  very superstitious
  courageous
  unimaginative

D despises weakness
  straightforward
  ambitious
  jealous
  impulsive
  cunning

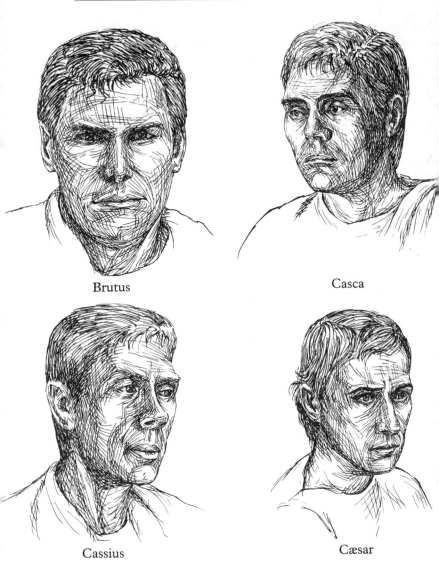

Brutus

Casca

Cassius

Cæsar

Quotations

The quotation, 'O he sits high in all the people's hearts', is said about Brutus. Which word from Brutus' list does it match best?

Make the same decision for the other characters with these quotations:

1 'such a man
  That is no fleering tell-tale.' (Casca)
2 'I tell thee what is to be feared
  Than what I fear; for always I am Cæsar.' (Cæsar)
3 'Such men as he be never at heart's ease
  Whiles they behold a greater than themselves.' (Cassius)

You now have the beginnings of four Character logs (see p230). As you read through the play, get into the habit of jotting down line references as you learn more about each character.

Brutus decides Cæsar must die because he fears Cæsar's ambition.

progress of the stars: the storm has obscured the stars
fault: disability
taper: candle
I know no … general: I have no personal reason to rebel against Cæsar; the only reason is for the general good of Rome.
would be: wants to be
It is the … walking: It is on bright days that poisonous snakes come out to bask in the sunshine and that is when you have to be careful where you tread.
disjoins Remorse from power: greatness is abused when power overrules feelings
and to speak … his reason: I admit he has always been reasonable

Act two

SCENE **1**

Brutus' orchard

Enter BRUTUS

BRUTUS What Lucius, ho!
I cannot, by the progress of the stars,
Give guess how near to day. Lucius I say!
I would it were my fault to sleep so soundly.
When Lucius, when? Awake, I say!
What Lucius!

Enter LUCIUS

LUCIUS Called you my lord?

BRUTUS Get me a taper in my study, Lucius:
When it is lighted, come and call me here.

LUCIUS I will my lord.

[*Exit*

BRUTUS It must be by his death; and for my part, 10
I know no personal cause to spurn at him,
But for the general. He would be crowned.
How that might change his nature, there's the
    question.
It is the bright day that brings forth the adder,
And that craves wary walking. Crown him that,
And then I grant we put a sting in him,
That at his will he may do danger with.
Th'abuse of greatness is, when it disjoins
Remorse from power; and to speak truth of
    Cæsar,
I have not known when his affections swayed 20
More than his reason. But 'tis a common proof,

Brutus is given one of the letters which Cassius has composed.

lowliness: humility, being respectful
young ambition's ladder: being humble is how an
    ambitious man starts his climb to the top
round: rung
base degrees: lower steps
Then lest ... prevent: So, in case he does, we must stop
    him
Will bear no colour: cannot be justified
Fashion it thus: Let's put it this way
that what he ... extremities: that if his present personal
    qualities develop and grow this is what he will become
kind: sort (like all snakes)
flint: (with which to light the taper)
calendar: we have heard much about Cæsar's faults, but
    little about the reforms he introduced. One reform was to
    the Roman calendar.
exhalations: meteors
redress: put things right
instigations: incitements, pleas to act

That lowliness is young ambition's ladder,
Whereto the climber-upward turns his face;
But when he once attains the upmost round,
He then unto the ladder turns his back,
Looks in the clouds, scorning the base degrees
By which he did ascend. So Cæsar may;
Then lest he may, prevent. And, since the quarrel
Will bear no colour for the thing he is,
Fashion it thus: that what he is, augmented,   30
Would run to these and these extremities.
And therefore think him as a serpent's egg,
Which hatched, would as his kind, grow
    mischievous,
And kill him in the shell.

Re-enter LUCIUS

LUCIUS   The taper burneth in your closet sir.
Searching the window for a flint, I found
This paper, thus sealed up; and I am sure
It did not lie there when I went to bed.

Gives him the letter

BRUTUS   Get you to bed again, it is not day.
Is not tomorrow, boy, the ides of March?   40
LUCIUS   I know not sir.
BRUTUS   Look in the calendar, and bring me word.
LUCIUS   I will sir.

[*Exit*

BRUTUS   The exhalations whizzing in the air
Give so much light that I may read by them.

Opens the letter and reads

'Brutus, thou sleep'st; awake, and see thyself.
Shall Rome, &c. Speak, strike, redress.'
'Brutus, thou sleep'st: awake!'
Such instigations have been often dropped

The letter reinforces Brutus' intentions. Cassius and others arrive.

piece it out: work it out (Brutus is intrigued by the form of the letter)

under one man's awe: fearful of one man

Tarquin: Tarquinius Superbus, the last man to be King of Rome, was driven out when the Republic was formed.

redress: putting things right

entreated: begged

O Rome ... Brutus: I promise you, Rome, that if the result is that things are put right, I will give you everything you ask.

whet: sharpen, focus

Between the acting ... insurrection: The interval between deciding to do something dreadful and carrying it out is like a nightmare. Man's spirit (conscience) and his impulses (what he feels like doing) are in conflict. A kind of war takes place in the mind, just as a kingdom is disturbed by a civil war.

brother: Cassius is married to Brutus' sister, Junia.

moe: more

Where I have took them up.   50
'Shall Rome &c.' Thus must I piece it out:
Shall Rome stand under one man's awe? What,
    Rome?
My ancestors did from the streets of Rome
The Tarquin drive, when he was called a king.
'Speak, strike, redress.' Am I entreated
To speak and strike? O Rome, I make thee
    promise,
If the redress will follow, thou receivest
Thy full petition at the hand of Brutus.

Re-enter LUCIUS

LUCIUS   Sir, March is wasted fifteen days.

Knocking within

BRUTUS   'Tis good. Go to the gate; somebody knocks.   60

                                              [*Exit Lucius*

Since Cassius first did whet me against Cæsar,
I have not slept.
Between the acting of a dreadful thing
And the first motion, all the interim is
Like a phantasma, or a hideous dream.
The genius and the mortal instruments
Are then in council; and the state of man,
Like to a little kingdom, suffers then
The nature of an insurrection.

Re-enter LUCIUS

LUCIUS   Sir, 'tis your brother Cassius at the door,   70
            Who doth desire to see you.

BRUTUS   Is he alone?

LUCIUS   No sir, there are moe with him.

BRUTUS   Do you know them?

LUCIUS   No sir, their hats are plucked about their ears,
            And half their faces buried in their cloaks,

Brutus is introduced to the conspirators.

mark of favour: feature
faction: group
Sham'st thou ... free: Are you ashamed to show yourself even at night when evil acts are performed?
visage: face
affability: pleasantness
native semblance: natural appearance
Erebus: dark route to hell
prevention: exposure
too bold ... rest: going too far in disturbing your sleep
What watchful ... night? What keeps you awake?

That by no means I may discover them
By any mark of favour.

BRUTUS   Let 'em enter.

                                    [*Exit Lucius*

They are the faction. O conspiracy,
Sham'st thou to show thy dangerous brow by
    night,
When evils are most free? O then, by day
Where wilt thou find a cavern dark enough   80
To mask thy monstrous visage? Seek none,
    conspiracy;
Hide it in smiles and affability.
For if thou put thy native semblance on,
Not Erebus itself were dim enough
To hide thee from prevention.

Enter the conspirators, CASSIUS, CASCA, DECIUS,
    CINNA, METELLUS CIMBER, *and* TREBONIUS

CASSIUS   I think we are too bold upon your rest.
Good morrow Brutus; do we trouble you?

BRUTUS   I have been up this hour, awake all night.
Know I these men that come along with you?

CASSIUS   Yes, every man of them; and no man here   90
But honours you; and every one doth wish
You had but that opinion of yourself
Which every noble Roman bears to you.
This is Trebonius.

BRUTUS   He is welcome hither.

CASSIUS   This, Decius Brutus.

BRUTUS   He is welcome too.

CASSIUS   This, Casca; this, Cinna; and this, Metellus
Cimber.

BRUTUS   They are all welcome.
What watchful cares do interpose themselves

Brutus joins the conspiracy but he will not take an oath. He says it is unnecessary for Romans.

Here lies the east: a necessary act to seal a Roman conspiracy was the oath, carried out when facing east.

fret: cut patterns into

Here as I point ... fire: Casca is pointing out that because it is early in the year, sunrise is quite late and therefore the sun rises between east and south. Later in the year, when sunrise is earlier, the sun will rise to the north of east.

Weighing: considering

resolution: agreement

If not the face ... bed: If the looks in men's faces, the way in which people are suffering, and what we have to put up with at the present time are not powerful reasons for action, then let's all go back to bed.

idle: empty

high-sighted: ambitious

lottery: chance

these: (things referred to in lines 114–115)

kindle: inspire

steel with valour: make courageous

spur: incentive (lines 123–124, riding metaphor)

prick us to redress: urge us to put things right

palter: say one thing and mean another

That this ... fall for it?: we shall succeed or die

cautelous: cautious, wary

carrions: 'dead-heads'

	Betwixt your eyes and night?
CASSIUS	Shall I entreat a word?

100

[BRUTUS *and* CASSIUS *whisper*

DECIUS	Here lies the east. Doth not the day break here?
CASCA	No.
CINNA	O pardon sir, it doth; and yon grey lines
	That fret the clouds are messengers of day.
CASCA	You shall confess that you are both deceived.
	Here, as I point my sword, the sun arises,
	Which is a great way growing on the south,
	Weighing the youthful season of the year.
	Some two months hence, up higher toward the north
	He first presents his fire; and the high east
	Stands, as the Capitol, directly here.
BRUTUS	Give me your hands all over, one by one.
CASSIUS	And let us swear our resolution.
BRUTUS	No, not an oath. If not the face of men,
	The sufferance of our souls, the time's abuse -
	If these be motives weak, break off betimes,
	And every man hence to his idle bed.
	So let high-sighted tyranny range on,
	Till each man drop by lottery. But if these,
	As I am sure they do, bear fire enough
	To kindle cowards, and to steel with valour
	The melting spirits of women, then, countrymen,
	What need we any spur but our own cause,
	To prick us to redress? What other bond
	Than secret Romans, that have spoke the word,
	And will not palter? And what other oath
	Than honesty to honesty engaged,
	That this shall be, or we will fall for it?
	Swear priests and cowards, and men cautelous,
	Old feeble carrions, and such suffering souls
	That welcome wrongs; unto bad causes swear

110

120

130

Brutus is alone in thinking that Cicero should not be approached to join the conspiracy, but the others readily agree. Brutus disagrees with Cassius who thinks that Antony should die as well as Cæsar.

even: steady
insuppressive mettle: nature which cannot be conquered
or ... or: either...or
Is guilty ... bastardy: every drop of blood becomes
    un-Roman.
no whit: not at all
break with: inform
shrewd contriver: one who manages things cunningly
and, you know ... us all: he has a position (as Consul)
    which could be improved to cause us much trouble
course: (of action)
wrath: anger, revenge

Such creatures as men doubt; but do not stain
The even virtue of our enterprise,
Nor th'insuppressive mettle of our spirits,
To think that or our cause or our performance
Did need an oath; when every drop of blood
That every Roman bears, and nobly bears,
Is guilty of a several bastardy,
If he do break the smallest particle
Of any promise that hath passed from him.   140

CASSIUS   But what of Cicero? Shall we sound him?
I think he will stand very strong with us.

CASCA   Let us not leave him out.

CINNA   No, by no means.

METELLUS   O let us have him, for his silver hairs
Will purchase us a good opinion
And buy men's voices to commend our deeds.
It shall be said his judgement ruled our hands;
Our youths and wildness shall no whit appear,
But all be buried in his gravity.

BRUTUS   O name him not; let us not break with him;   150
For he will never follow any thing
That other men begin.

CASSIUS   Then leave him out.

CASCA   Indeed he is not fit.

DECIUS   Shall no man else be touched but only Cæsar?

CASSIUS   Decius, well urged. I think it is not meet,
Mark Antony, so well beloved of Cæsar,
Should outlive Cæsar. We shall find of him
A shrewd contriver; and you know, his means,
If he improve them, may well stretch so far
As to annoy us all; which to prevent,   160
Let Antony and Cæsar fall together.

BRUTUS   Our course will seem too bloody, Caius Cassius,
To cut the head off, and then hack the limbs,
Like wrath in death, and envy afterwards;

Brutus says that Antony will be no danger to them. Cassius is much less sure. They all agree that Antony shall live.

Let us be sacrificers but not butchers: Cæsar must die for the people's good but it is not necessary for anyone else to die

hew: hack

And let our hearts ... chide 'em: let our feelings work us up into a rage, just as masters urge their servants on to act, and then let us appear to regret it, just as the masters blame the servants for what they have done.

purpose: what we intend to do

purgers: cleansers; those who remove something unpleasant

ingrafted: deep-rooted

take thought ... Cæsar: commit suicide

that were much he should: he will hardly do that

For Antony is but a limb of Cæsar.
Let us be sacrificers, but not butchers, Caius.
We all stand up against the spirit of Cæsar,
And in the spirit of men there is no blood:
O that we then could come by Cæsar's spirit,
And not dismember Cæsar! But alas,   170
Cæsar must bleed for it. And gentle friends,
Let's kill him boldly, but not wrathfully;
Let's carve him as a dish fit for the gods,
Not hew him as a carcass fit for hounds.
And let our hearts, as subtle masters do,
Stir up their servants to an act of rage,
And after seem to chide 'em. This shall make
Our purpose necessary, and not envious;
Which so appearing to the common eyes,
We shall be called purgers, not murderers.   180
And for Mark Antony, think not of him;
For he can do no more than Cæsar's arm
When Cæsar's head is off.

CASSIUS   Yet I fear him;
For in the ingrafted love he bears to Cæsar -

BRUTUS   Alas good Cassius, do not think of him.
If he love Cæsar, all that he can do
Is to himself, take thought, and die for Cæsar.
And that were much he should; for he is given
To sports, to wildness, and much company.

TREBONIUS   There is no fear in him; let him not die,   190
For he will live, and laugh at this hereafter.

Clock strikes

BRUTUS   Peace, count the clock.

CASSIUS   The clock hath stricken three.

TREBONIUS   'Tis time to part.

CASSIUS   But it is doubtful yet,
Whether Cæsar will come forth today or no;
For he is superstitious grown of late,

Cassius worries that Cæsar might stay at home.
Decius says he can persuade Cæsar to attend the
Senate. They all arrange to meet at Cæsar's house.

main opinion: personal belief
apparent prodigies: omens which have appeared
augurers: officials who advised on whether certain days
   would prove to be lucky or unlucky
resolved: determined
o'ersway him: make him change his mind
unicorns ... flatterers: there are many ways to trap
   animals - and men can be trapped by flattery
For I can ... bent: I can put him in the right frame of mind
uttermost: latest
bear Cæsar hard: has a grudge against Cæsar
rated him: told him off
by him: to him
fashion: work on, persuade
put on: show
constancy: consistency

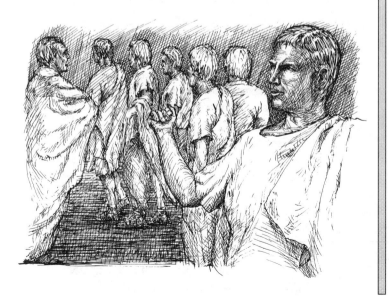

	Quite from the main opinion he held once	
	Of fantasy, of dreams, and ceremonies.	
	It may be, these apparent prodigies,	
	The unaccustomed terror of this night,	
	And the persuasion of his augurers,	200
	May hold him from the Capitol today.	
DECIUS	Never fear that. If he be so resolved,	
	I can o'ersway him; for he loves to hear	
	That unicorns may be betrayed with trees,	
	And bears with glasses, elephants with holes,	
	Lions with toils, and men with flatterers;	
	But when I tell him he hates flatterers,	
	He says he does, being then most flattered.	
	Let me work;	
	For I can give his humour the true bent,	210
	And I will bring him to the Capitol.	
CASSIUS	Nay, we will all of us be there to fetch him.	
BRUTUS	By the eighth hour; is that the uttermost?	
CINNA	Be that the uttermost, and fail not then.	
METELLUS	Caius Ligarius doth bear Cæsar hard,	
	Who rated him for speaking well of Pompey;	
	I wonder none of you have thought of him.	
BRUTUS	Now good Metellus, go along by him.	
	He loves me well, and I have given him reasons.	
	Send him but hither, and I'll fashion him.	220
CASSIUS	The morning comes upon's. We'll leave you, Brutus.	
	And friends disperse yourselves; but all remember	
	What you have said, and show yourselves true Romans.	
BRUTUS	Good gentlemen, look fresh and merrily.	
	Let not our looks put on our purposes,	
	But bear it as our Roman actors do,	
	With untired spirits and formal constancy;	
	And so good morrow to you everyone.	

Brutus' wife, Portia, is worried by his behaviour. He says that he is unwell.

honey-heavy: sweet
figures … fantasies: dreams
Musing: thinking, worrying
wafture: wave
enkindled: burning
humour: temporary mood
And could it work … Brutus: If your outward appearance were to change as much as your mental state then I should not be able to recognise you
embrace … by it: do something about it

[Exeunt all but Brutus

Boy! Lucius! Fast asleep? It is no matter;
Enjoy the honey-heavy dew of slumber.   230
Thou hast no figures nor no fantasies,
Which busy care draws in the brains of men;
Therefore thou sleep'st so sound.

Enter PORTIA

PORTIA   Brutus my lord.

BRUTUS Portia! What mean you? Wherefore rise you now?
It is not for your health thus to commit
Your weak condition to the raw cold morning.

PORTIA Nor for yours neither. Y'have ungently, Brutus,
Stole from my bed: and yesternight at supper
You suddenly arose, and walked about,
Musing and sighing, with your arms across;   240
And when I asked you what the matter was,
You stared upon me with ungentle looks.
I urged you further; then you scratched your head,
And too impatiently stamped your foot.
Yet I insisted, yet you answered not,
But with an angry wafture of your hand
Gave sign for me to leave you. So I did,
Fearing to strengthen that impatience
Which seemed too much enkindled, and withal
Hoping it was but an effect of humour,   250
Which sometime hath his hour with every man.
It will not let you eat, nor talk, nor sleep;
And could it work so much upon your shape,
As it hath much prevailed on your condition,
I should not know you Brutus. Dear my lord,
Make me acquainted with your cause of grief.

BRUTUS I am not well in health, and that is all.

PORTIA Brutus is wise, and were he not in health,
He would embrace the means to come by it.

BRUTUS Why so I do. Good Portia go to bed.   260

**Portia demands to know what is troubling her
husband. She begs him to tell her the truth.**

physical: a cure
unbraced: in loosened clothing
humours: dampness
dare the vile contagion: risk disease, serious illness
rheumy: likely to give catarrh
unpurged: unclean, poisonous
by the right ... place: by the rights I have as your wife
charm: beg
great vow: marriage vow
heavy: distressed, have a weight on your mind
had resort to: been to see
Is it excepted: is there an exception that
appertain: refer
Am I ... limitation: Are we one only within limits (when it
   suits you)?
suburbs: fringes
harlot: mistress
ruddy drops: blood

PORTIA	Is Brutus sick, and is it physical
	To walk unbraced and suck up the humours
	Of the dank morning? What, is Brutus sick?
	And will he steal out of his wholesome bed,
	To dare the vile contagion of the night,
	And tempt the rheumy and unpurged air,
	To add unto his sickness? No my Brutus,
	You have some sick offence within your mind,
	Which, by the right and virtue of my place,
	I ought to know of: and upon my knees,
	I charm you, by my once commended beauty,
	By all your vows of love, and that great vow
	Which did incorporate and make us one,
	That you unfold to me, your self, your half,
	Why you are heavy, and what men tonight
	Have had resort to you; for here have been
	Some six or seven, who did hide their faces
	Even from darkness.
BRUTUS	Kneel not, gentle Portia.
PORTIA	I should not need, if you were gentle Brutus.
	Within the bond of marriage, tell me Brutus,
	Is it excepted I should know no secrets
	That appertain to you? Am I your self
	But as it were in sort or limitation,
	To keep with you at meals, comfort your bed,
	And talk to you sometimes? Dwell I but in the suburbs
	Of your good pleasure? If it be no more,
	Portia is Brutus' harlot, not his wife.
BRUTUS	You are my true and honourable wife,
	As dear to me as are the ruddy drops
	That visit my sad heart.
PORTIA	If this were true, then should I know this secret.
	I grant I am a woman; but withal
	A woman that Lord Brutus took to wife.
	I grant I am a woman; but withal

270

280

290

Portia has wounded herself to prove her loyalty to
Brutus. He promises to tell her everything. Caius
Ligarius arrives and, although sick, pledges his
support.

well-reputed: well thought of
Cato: Cato was the fourth generation of a well-known
  Republican family. He fought for Pompey against Cæsar
  and committed suicide rather than surrender. He was
  much admired by Brutus.
counsels: thoughts
disclose: reveal
constancy: loyalty
Render: make
partake: share
engagements: dealings
construe: make known
charactery: writing (i.e.what you have read in my looks)
Vouchsafe: I give you
kerchief: Ligarius was very ill and had a scarf or cloth over
  his nose and mouth
would: I wish
exploit: deed
had you: if you had
derived ... loins: from a worthy family

A woman well-reputed, Cato's daughter.
Think you I am no stronger than my sex,
Being so fathered, and so husbanded?
Tell me your counsels, I will not disclose 'em.
I have made strong proof of my constancy,
Giving myself a voluntary wound   300
Here in the thigh. Can I bear that with patience,
And not my husband's secrets?

BRUTUS   O ye gods.
Render me worthy of this noble wife!

Knocking within

Hark, hark, one knocks. Portia go in awhile,
And by and by thy bosom shall partake
The secrets of my heart.
All my engagements I will construe to thee,
All the charactery of my sad brows.
Leave me with haste.

                          [*Exit Portia*

                  Lucius, who's that knocks?

Re-enter LUCIUS *and* LIGARIUS

LUCIUS	He is a sick man that would speak with you. 310
BRUTUS	Caius Ligarius, that Metellus spake of.
	Boy, stand aside. Caius Ligarius, how?
LIGARIUS	Vouchsafe good morrow from a feeble tongue.
BRUTUS	O what a time you have chose out brave Caius,
	To wear a kerchief! Would you were not sick!
LIGARIUS	I am not sick, if Brutus have in hand
	Any exploit worthy the name of honour.
BRUTUS	Such an exploit have I in hand Ligarius,
	Had you a healthful ear to hear of it.
LIGARIUS	By all the gods that Romans bow before, 320
	I here discard my sickness. Soul of Rome,
	Brave son, derived from honourable loins,

Brutus and Ligarius leave to join the other conspirators.

unfold: reveal
sufficeth: is enough
exorcist: one who drives out evil spirits
conjured up: revived
mortified: dead

ACTIVITIES

Keeping track

1 What has Brutus decided?
2 According to Brutus, what is the best way for the conspirators to keep their secret safe?
3 What reason does Brutus give for not taking the oath?
4 Why are the other conspirators so ready to agree with Brutus about Cicero?
5 What is Brutus' opinion of Antony?
6 What arguments does Portia use to try to persuade Brutus to tell her what is troubling him?

	Thou like an exorcist hast conjured up
	My mortified spirit. Now bid me run,
	And I will strive with things impossible,
	Yea get the better of them. What's to do?
BRUTUS	A piece of work that will make sick men whole.
LIGARIUS	But are not some whole that we must make sick?
BRUTUS	That must we also. What it is, my Caius,
	I shall unfold to thee, as we are going 330
	To whom it must be done.

LIGARIUS   Set on your foot,
And with a heart new-fired I follow you,
To do I know not what; but it sufficeth
That Brutus leads me on.

BRUTUS   Follow me then.

[*Exeunt*

Discussion

1 What is Cassius likely to be telling Brutus in their
   whispered conversation (line 100)? Would Brutus have any
   questions to ask?
2 Portia uses the words 'ungently' and 'ungentle' when she
   speaks of Brutus' behaviour. What does this tell us about
   the way in which Brutus usually behaves towards her?
3 What are Brutus' feelings for Portia?
4 Why does he keep his secret from her?
5 What makes him change his mind?
6 Do you think he has made the right decision?

Drama

The conspirators

Groups of 8.

You have been commissioned as actors to pose for a painting entitled 'The Conspirators'.

1 Read Brutus' speech 'No, not an oath' lines 114 - 140.
2 Discuss where and how the seven conspirators will be standing, gesturing, looking etc.
3 The eighth member of your group composes your picture. S/he stands back from time to time to adjust your positions to get the appropriate effect.
4 Try to get variety into the picture - invent looks and glances which capture the tension, the excitement and doubts on their faces, in their eyes and bodies.
5 When your picture is ready, submit it to the rest of the class.
6 Discuss the portrait each group has produced.

Follow up.
1 Draw or photograph the pictures.
2 Consider what difference it makes if the commissioner of the portrait was any of the following:
Mark Antony, Calphurnia, Portia, one of the conspirators, Octavius.
Each group could have a different commissioner. Compare the differences.

Character

1 From a soliloquy we learn a lot about the speaker because we know s/he is saying what s/he really feels. There is no one else present to impress or deceive. What do we find out about Brutus from his soliloquy in lines 10-34?
2 Bring your Character logs on Brutus, Cassius, Cæsar, and Casca up to date.
3 Antony is discussed in lines 155-160, 165 and 181-191. There is some disagreement amongst those discussing him,

and it will be interesting later to look back and see who is most accurate. Begin a Character log for Antony.

Close study

In Brutus' speech, lines 162-183, he is replying to a suggestion made by Cassius.

1 What has Cassius suggested?
2 What does Brutus think of Antony?
3 Brutus says, 'But alas, Cæsar must bleed for it.' What does he think of Cæsar?
4 Are there any other lines from which we can work out Brutus' feelings for Cæsar?
5 Which line shows us that Brutus is concerned about what people will think?
6 What do you notice about the language of these lines?
   ● 'Let us be sacrificers, but not butchers'
   ● 'Let's kill him boldly, but not wrathfully'
   ● 'We shall be called purgers, not murderers'
     (This will be referred to again, later.)

Writing

For Lucius the events of Act 2 scene 1 have been most unusual. He has not been present all the time, and has even been asleep, but he must have seen and heard enough to be curious, at least. As Lucius, write part of a diary which covers the events of this scene.

Quiz

Who said the following, and to whom?
1 '... those sparks of life
   That should be in a Roman you do want ...'
2 'What need we any spur but our own cause
   To prick us to redress?'
3 'Make me acquainted with your cause of grief'

Who said the following about whom?

4 'A man no mightier than thyself, or me,
   In personal action, yet prodigious grown'

5 'Him and his worth, and our great need of him
   You have right well conceited.'

6 'I know no personal cause to spurn at him
   But for the general'

**Cæsar's wife, Calphurnia, has had a restless night.
She urges him to stay at home.**

within: inside (the servant would be in an inner room)
priests: augurers, referred to in Act 2 scene 1
present: immediate
opinions of success: today's forecast
The things … my back: people only challenge me behind
   my back
stood on ceremonies: relied on omens
watch: security men who patrolled the streets at night

Do you remember?

7 Whose calm behaviour in the storm contrasted with
Casca's uncontrolled fear?

8 Who were the men whom the conspirators wanted
a) included in the conspiracy;
b) killed at the same time as Cæsar?

9 Who made a rapid recovery from illness to join the conspiracy?

10 Who were the eight conspirators?

SCENE **2**

Cæsar's house
Thunder and lightning. Enter CÆSAR *in his nightgown.*

CÆSAR   Nor heaven nor earth have been at peace tonight.
Thrice hath Calphurnia in her sleep cried out,
'Help ho, they murder Cæsar!' Who's within?

Enter a SERVANT

SERVANT   My lord.

CÆSAR   Go bid the priests do present sacrifice,
And bring me their opinions of success.

SERVANT   I will my lord.   [*Exit*

Enter CALPHURNIA

CALPHURNIA   What mean you Cæsar? Think you to walk forth?
You shall not stir out of your house today.

CÆSAR   Cæsar shall forth. The things that threatened me   10
Ne'er looked but on my back; when they shall see
The face of Cæsar, they are vanished.

CALPHURNIA   Cæsar, I never stood on ceremonies,
Yet now they fright me. There is one within,
Besides the things that we have heard and seen,
Recounts most horrid sights seen by the watch.

Despite Calphurnia's pleading, Cæsar says he will go to the Senate.

whelped: given birth
beyond all use: outside the normal, usual, run of things
purposed: decided
Are to the world ... Cæsar: are as much about the whole world as they are about Cæsar
necessary: unavoidable
entrails: guts
in shame of cowardice: to put cowards to shame

A lioness hath whelped in the streets,
And graves have yawned, and yielded up their dead;
Fierce fiery warriors fought upon the clouds
In ranks and squadrons and right form of war, 20
Which drizzled blood upon the Capitol.
The noise of battle hurtled in the air;
Horses did neigh, and dying men did groan,
And ghosts did shriek and squeal about the
    streets.
O Cæsar, these things are beyond all use,
And I do fear them.

CÆSAR   What can be avoided
Whose end is purposed by the mighty gods?
Yet Cæsar shall go forth; for these predictions
Are to the world in general as to Cæsar.

CALPHURNIA When beggars die, there are no comets seen; 30
The heavens themselves blaze forth the death of
    princes.

CÆSAR Cowards die many times before their deaths,
The valiant never taste of death but once.
Of all the wonders that I yet have heard,
It seems to me most strange that men should
    fear,
Seeing that death, a necessary end,
Will come when it will come.

Enter SERVANT

                    What say the augurers?

SERVANT They would not have you to stir forth today.
Plucking the entrails of an offering forth,
They could not find a heart within the beast. 40

CÆSAR The gods do this in shame of cowardice.
Cæsar should be a beast without a heart
If he should stay at home today for fear.
No Cæsar shall not. Danger knows full well
That Cæsar is more dangerous than he.

Cæsar gives in to Calphurnia and agrees to stay at home. Decius is told to inform the Senate that Cæsar will not attend that day. He asks for a reason. Caesar tells him about a dream Calphurnia has had.

Your wisdom is ... confidence: you are so self-assured you are not being sensible
Let me ... prevail: let me have my own way
for thy humour: to please you
very happy: good
graybeards: old men
cause: reason
The cause is in my will: That is what I want!
stays: keeps

We are two lions littered in one day,
And I the elder and more terrible.
And Cæsar shall go forth.

CALPHURNIA   Alas, my lord,
Your wisdom is consumed in confidence.
Do not go forth today. Call it my fear   50
That keeps you in the house, and not your own.
We'll send Mark Antony to the Senate House,
And he shall say you are not well today.
Let me upon my knee prevail in this.

CÆSAR   Mark Antony shall say I am not well,
And for thy humour I will stay at home.

Enter DECIUS

Here's Decius Brutus, he shall tell them so.

DECIUS   Cæsar, all hail. Good morrow worthy Cæsar.
I come to fetch you to the Senate House.

CÆSAR   And you are come in very happy time   60
To bear my greetings to the senators,
And tell them that I will not come today.
Cannot, is false; and that I dare not, falser;
I will not come today. Tell them so Decius.

CALPHURNIA Say he is sick.

CÆSAR   Shall Cæsar send a lie?
Have I in conquest streched mine arm so far
To be afeard to tell graybeards the truth?
Decius, go tell them Cæsar will not come.

DECIUS   Most mighty Cæsar, let me know some cause,
Lest I be laughed at when I tell them so.   70

CÆSAR   The cause is in my will; I will not come;
That is enough to satisfy the senate.
But for your private satisfaction,
Because I love you, I will let you know.
Calphurnia here, my wife, stays me at home.
She dreamt tonight she saw my statue,

Decius interprets Calphurnia's dream to Cæsar's satisfaction, and then says the Senate intend to crown Cæsar. Cæsar changes his mind again and decides to go. The conspirators arrive.

apply: interpret
imminent: about to happen
amiss: wrong(ly)
fair and fortunate: favourable
great Rome ... and cognizance: great Romans will crowd around to get something stained with this blood so it would act as a kind of memento. (In medieval times where a martyr died people were eager to claim a momento or 'relic'.)
expounded: explained
when you. .. say: what I have to say will prove it
concluded: decided
a mock ... rendered: someone is likely to say, scornfully
proceeding: actions
And reason ... liable: I always do things according to my love

	Which like a fountain with an hundred spouts
	Did run pure blood; and many lusty Romans
	Came smiling, and did bathe their hands in it.
	And these does she apply for warnings and
	portents 80
	Of evils imminent; and on her knee
	Hath begged that I will stay at home today.
DECIUS	This dream is all amiss interpreted;
	It was a vision fair and fortunate.
	Your statue spouting blood in many pipes,
	In which so many smiling Romans bathed,
	Signifies that from you great Rome shall suck
	Reviving blood, and that great men shall press
	For tinctures, stains, relics, and cognizance.
	This by Calphurnia's dream is signified. 90
CÆSAR	And this way have you well expounded it.
DECIUS	I have, when you have heard what I can say;
	And know it now: the senate have concluded
	To give this day a crown to mighty Cæsar.
	If you shall send them word you will not come,
	Their minds may change. Besides, it were a mock
	Apt to be rendered for some one to say,
	'Break up the senate till another time,
	When Cæsar's wife shall meet with better dreams.'
	If Cæsar hide himself, shall they not whisper, 100
	'Lo Cæsar is afraid'?
	Pardon me Cæsar, for my dear dear love
	To your proceeding bids me tell you this;
	And reason to my love is liable.
CÆSAR	How foolish do your fears seem now Calphurnia!
	I am ashamed I did yield to them.
	Give me my robe, for I will go.

Enter BRUTUS, LIGARIUS, METELLUS, CASCA,
TREBONIUS, CINNA *and* PUBLIUS

And look where Publius is come to fetch me.

Whilst Cæsar makes ready to leave, the conspirators confide their intentions.

ague: fever
notwithstanding: even so
so: and the same
every like: Brutus refers to Cæsar's 'like friends' in the line above.
yearns: grieves

PUBLIUS	Good morrow Cæsar.
CÆSAR	Welcome Publius.

What, Brutus, are you stirred so early too? 110
Good morrow Casca. Caius Ligarius,
Cæsar was ne'er so much your enemy
As that same ague which hath made you lean.
What is't o'clock?

BRUTUS	Cæsar, 'tis strucken eight.
CÆSAR	I thank you for your pains and courtesy.

Enter ANTONY

See, Antony, that revels long a-nights,
Is notwithstanding up. Good morrow Antony.

ANTONY   So to most noble Cæsar.

CÆSAR   Bid them prepare within.
I am to blame to be thus waited for.
Now Cinna; now, Metellus; what, Trebonius. 120
I have an hour's talk in store for you;
Remember that you call on me today.
Be near me, that I may remember you.

TREBONIUS   Cæsar I will: [*Aside*] and so near will I be,
That your best friends shall wish I had been
    further.

CÆSAR   Good friends go in, and taste some wine with me;
And we, like friends, will straightway go together.

BRUTUS   [*Aside*] That every like is not the same, O Cæsar,
The heart of Brutus yearns to think upon.

[*Exeunt*

Artemidorus reads out a warning message which he means to give to Cæsar.

1 Artemidorus reads out a message which names all the conspirators, and warns Cæsar about them. He is waiting to hand the note to Cæsar, and hoping that it will be read in time to save him.

Portia is extremely agitated. She wants Lucius to go to the Senate House, but she cannot tell him why.

1 Portia urges Lucius to hurry to the Senate House.
2 Lucius asks why he is going.
3 Portia says he must go and return, and then she can tell him what to do.

SCENE **3**

Rome. A street.
Enter ARTEMIDORUS *reading a paper*

ARTEMIDORUS 'Cæsar, beware of Brutus; take heed of Cassius;
come not near Casca; have an eye to Cinna;
trust not Trebonius; mark well Metellus
Cimber; Decius Brutus loves thee not; thou
hast wronged Caius Ligarius. There is but one
mind in all these men, and it is bent against
Cæsar. If thou beest not immortal, look about
you. Security gives way to conspiracy. The
mighty gods defend thee. Thy lover,
                    Artemidorus.' 10
Here will I stand till Cæsar pass along,
And as a suitor will I give him this.
My heart laments that virtue cannot live
Out of the teeth of emulation.
If thou read this, O Cæsar, thou mayst live;
If not, the Fates with traitors do contrive.

                                     [*Exit*

SCENE **4**

Rome A street.
Enter PORTIA *and* LUCIUS

PORTIA   I prithee boy, run to the Senate House;
Stay not to answer me, but get thee gone.
Why dost thou stay?

LUCIUS   To know my errand madam.

PORTIA   I would have had thee there and here again,
Ere I can tell thee what thou shouldst do there.

The soothsayer foresees danger for Cæsar.

4   Portia is finding it hard not to give away the secret.

5   Lucius is still puzzled.

6   Portia tells him to keep an eye on Brutus, who is not well, and to watch Cæsar carefully to see who approaches him. She hears the noise of a crowd from the direction of the Capitol.

7   Lucius cannot hear it.

8   On edge, Portia begins asking the Soothsayer for information.

9   Portia is anxious to learn if the Soothsayer knows the whereabouts of Cæsar; and if he has a message for Cæsar.

10   The Soothsayer has a message, and he says that Cæsar would be wise to listen to him. He does not know for certain, but he fears that Cæsar is in danger.

O constancy, be strong upon my side,
Set a huge mountain 'tween my heart and tongue.
I have a man's mind, but a woman's might.
How hard it is for women to keep counsel!
Art thou here yet?

LUCIUS   Madam, what should I do?   10
Run to the Capitol, and nothing else?
And so return to you, and nothing else?

PORTIA   Yes, bring me word boy, if thy lord look well,
For he went sickly forth; and take good note
What Cæsar doth, what suitors press to him.
Hark boy, what noise is that?

LUCIUS   I hear none madam,

PORTIA   Prithee listen well.
I heard a bustling rumour, like a fray,
And the wind brings it from the Capitol.

LUCIUS   Sooth madam, I hear nothing.   20

Enter the SOOTHSAYER

PORTIA   Come hither fellow. Which way hast thou been?

SOOTHSAYER At mine own house, good lady.

PORTIA   What is't aclock?

SOOTHSAYER About the ninth hour lady.

PORTIA   Is Cæsar yet gone to the Capitol?

SOOTHSAYER Madam not yet, I go to take my stand,
To see him pass on to the Capitol.

PORTIA   Thou hast some suit to Cæsar, has thou not?

SOOTHSAYER That I have lady, if it will please Cæsar
To be so good to Cæsar as to hear me,
I shall beseech him to befriend himself.   30

PORTIA   Why, know'st thou any harm's intended towards
                him?

SOOTHSAYER None that I know will be, much that I fear may
                chance.

What the Soothsayer tells Portia increases her fears.

11

11 The Soothsayer moves away to find a place less
    crowded so that Cæsar will hear him.

12 Portia bemoans her own weakness in being unable to
    stand the strain. She wishes the gods on Brutus' side.
    She tells Lucius, above the growing noise of the
    crowd, that Brutus has a plea to present to Cæsar,
    because she fears that Lucius has overheard her
    earlier remarks. At last she has orders for Lucius:
    'Tell Brutus I am well and bring back his reply.'

12

ACTIVITIES

Keeping track

1 What is the disagreement between Cæsar and
   Calphurnia?

2 Cæsar's change of mind appears sudden. What has
   made him decide to stay at home?

3 What are the two main arguments used by Decius to
   persuade Cæsar to change his mind yet again?

4 How is Brutus' attitude to the assassination
   emphasised here?

5 How do you think Artemidorus has come by such
   detailed information about the conspiracy?

6 Portia says, 'How hard it is for women to keep
   counsel'. Ignoring the sexism of this remark, how does
   it contradict what she has said previously?

Good morrow to you. Here the street is narrow.
The throng that follows Cæsar at the heels,
Of senators, of prætors, common suitors,
Will crowd a feeble man almost to death.
I'll get me to a place more void, and there
Speak to great Cæsar as he comes along.

[*Exit*

PORTIA   I must go in. Ay me, how weak a thing
The heart of woman is! O Brutus,   40
The heavens speed thee in thine enterprise.
Sure the boy heard me. Brutus hath a suit
That Cæsar will not grant. O, I grow faint.
Run Lucius, and commend me to my lord;
Say I am merry. Come to me again,
And bring me word what he doth say to thee.

[*Exeunt severally*

Discussion

1 'Cowards die many times before their deaths,
   The valiant never taste of death but once.'
   What does Cæsar mean? Is he right?
2 We have seen both Portia and Calphurnia in conversation
   with their husbands. How similar do the ladies appear, and
   how different? How are they regarded by their husbands? Is
   this because of the characters of the husbands, or the
   characters of the wives; or both?
3 In Act 2 scene 4, because there are no stage directions we
   have to work out for ourselves whether Portia is speaking to
   herself, talking in a normal voice, or shouting above the
   noise of the crowd. Look at lines 4-10 and 39-46 and
   decide how they would be spoken.

Drama

How weak a thing the heart of woman is!

Divide the class into boys and girls.

The boys divide into 2 groups - A and B.

The girls divide into 2 groups - C and D.

Women have often been left behind while men go out to fight or get involved in terrible events. Calphurnia and Portia could be portrayed as 'weak hearted things', but they could also be played as stronger or less sympathetic women; even women who are annoyed by their husbands' secrecy and pigheadedness - although they still love them.

Group A - recreate the portrait of 'The Conspirators' (see p88)

Group B - recreate the statue of Cæsar (see p46)

Group C - adopt the roles of Portia and her friends who are discussing the Conspirators (Group A)

Group D - adopt the roles of Calphurnia and her friends who are discussing the obstinacy of Cæsar.

Class activity

Now share your work with the rest of the class.

Character

1 Cassius has said that Cæsar thinks of himself as a god. Brutus has said that Cæsar is ambitious. Are there any signs in Act 2 scene 2 that one, or both, of these judgments is/are accurate?

2 Artemidorus expects Cæsar to accept the warning note as he passes by. We are told suitors will present their pleas to Cæsar personally. From what you know about Cæsar, do you think this means that he is really approachable; or is he only pretending to listen to the common man?

3 Bring up to date your Character logs on Brutus, Cassius, Cæsar, Casca and Antony.

Close study

1 Cæsar refers to himself as 'Cæsar' on some occasions, and

'I' on others. When does he use each form of reference?
Can you suggest why he should ever use 'Cæsar' when
speaking of himself?

2 At the end of Act 2 scene 2 Cæsar says:'
Remember that you call on me today.
Be near me, that I may remember you.'
- What does Cæsar mean?
- What do the conspirators think?
- What are we, the audience, thinking?

Writing

Opposition to Cæsar has to be secret, it cannot be openly
declared. As Caius Ligarius, write a short letter to a friend
outside Rome explaining your concern at the political
situation. You can include your own attitude to Cæsar (see
Act 2 scene 1 lines 215-216) and the attitude of others, but it
could prove dangerous to name names.

Quiz

Who said the following, and to whom?
1 'You shall not stir out of your house today'
2 'for thy humour I will stay at home'
3 'I will not come;
That is enough to satisfy the senate'

Who said the following about whom?
4 'She dreamt tonight she saw my statue,
Which like a fountain with an hundred spouts
Did run pure blood'
5 'If you shall send them word you will not come,
Their minds may change'
6 'and so near will I be,
That your best friends shall wish I had been further'

Do you remember?
7 What the augurers interpreted as an ill omen?

Cæsar ignores two warnings. Cassius fears the plot has been discovered.

schedule: scroll
Trebonius . . . suit: (Decius distracts Cæsar's attention)
That touches Cæsar nearer: that is of greater concern to Cæsar personally
What, is the fellow mad?: (Cæsar dismisses Artemidorus from his mind, and his own fate is sealed)
give place: move aside
enterprise: plan

Act three

SCENE **1**

Rome before the Capitol.
A crowd of people; among them ARTEMIDORUS *and
the* SOOTHSAYER. *Flourish. Enter* CÆSAR, BRUTUS,
CASSIUS, CASCA, DECIUS, METELLUS, TREBONIUS,
CINNA, ANTONY, LEPIDUS, POPILIUS, PUBLIUS, *and
others*

CÆSAR	The ides of March are come.
SOOTHSAYER	Ay Cæsar, but not gone.
ARTEMIDORUS	Hail Cæsar. Read this schedule.
DECIUS	Trebonius doth desire you to o'er-read At your best leisure this his humble suit.
ARTEMIDORUS	O Cæsar, read mine first; for mine's a suit That touches Cæsar nearer. Read it great Cæsar.
CÆSAR	What touches us ourself shall be least served.
ARTEMIDORUS	Delay not Cæsar, read it instantly.
CÆSAR	What, is the fellow mad?
PUBLIUS	Sirrah, give place.
CASSIUS	What, urge you your petitions in the street? Come to the Capitol.

10

CÆSAR *and the rest enter the Senate*

POPILIUS	I wish your enterprise today may thrive.
CASSIUS	What enterprise Popilius?
POPILIUS	Fare you well.
BRUTUS	What said Popilius Lena?
CASSIUS	He wished today our enterprise might thrive. I fear our purpose is discovered.
BRUTUS	Look how he makes to Cæsar. Mark him.

The secret is safe. According to plan, Antony is distracted. Metellus pleads for his brother's return from exile but Cæsar is unmoved.

we fear prevention: we are afraid we might be stopped

Cassius or Cæsar . . . back: Either Cassius or Cæsar will not return alive

be constant: pull yourself together

presently: at once

addressed: in position

redress: put right

puissant: powerful

prevent: anticipate

couchings and these lowly courtesies: bowing and scraping

turn pre-ordinance . . . law of children: alter the law of destiny, established at the beginning of time, to ever-changing rules of a children's game

fond: foolish

spaniel: like a dog

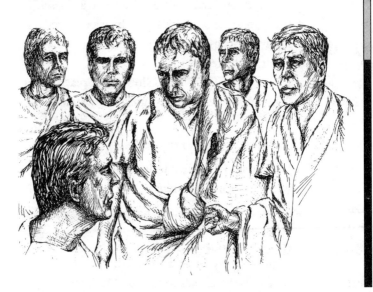

CASSIUS	Casca, be sudden, for we fear prevention.
	Brutus, what shall be done? If this be known, 20
	Cassius or Cæsar never shall turn back,
	For I will slay myself.
BRUTUS	Cassius be constant.
	Popilius Lena speaks not of our purposes,
	For look, he smiles, and Cæsar doth not change.
CASSIUS	Trebonius knows his time; for look you Brutus,
	He draws Mark Antony out of the way.

                      [Exeunt Antony and Trebonius

DECIUS	Where is Metellus Cimber? Let him go.
	And presently prefer his suit to Cæsar.
BRUTUS	He is addressed; press near and second him.
CINNA	Casca, you are the first that rears your hand. 30
CÆSAR	Are we all ready? What is now amiss
	That Cæsar and his senate must redress?
METELLUS	Most high, most mighty, and most puissant Cæsar,
	Metellus Cimber throws before thy seat
	An humble heart. *[Kneeling]*
CÆSAR	I must prevent thee Cimber.
	These couchings, and these lowly courtesies
	Might fire the blood of ordinary men,
	And turn pre-ordinance and first decree
	Into the law of children. Be not fond,
	To think that Cæsar bears such rebel blood 40
	That will be thawed from the true quality
	With that which melteth fools; I mean sweet words,
	Low-crooked curtsies, and base spaniel fawning.
	Thy brother by decree is banished.
	If thou dost bend, and pray, and fawn for him,
	I spurn thee like a cur out of my way.
	Know, Cæsar doth not wrong, nor without cause

Brutus and Cassius support Metellus' case, but Cæsar will not be moved. The conspirators close round Cæsar, as if pleading with him. They kill Cæsar.

enfranchisement: the right of a Roman citizen
If I could . . . move me: if there were some higher authority to whom I could pray for change, then perhaps you could change me
firmament: sky
sparks: stars
apprehensive: fearful
unassailable holds on his rank: keeps his position, unchallenged
constant: firm
Hence!: Go away
Olympus: mountain in Greece, home of the gods
Brutus: Decius Brutus
bootless: in vain
Et tu, Brute?: And you (Even you), Brutus?

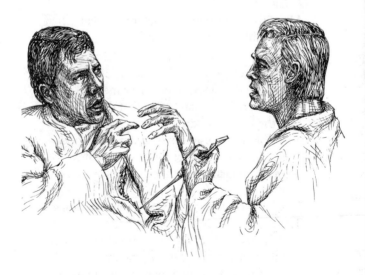

	Will he be satisfied.	
METELLUS	Is there no voice more worthy than my own,	
	To sound more sweetly in great Cæsar's ear	50
	For the repealing of my banished brother?	
BRUTUS	I kiss thy hand, but not in flattery Cæsar;	
	Desiring thee that Publius Cimber may	
	Have an immediate freedom of repeal.	
CÆSAR	What, Brutus?	
CASSIUS	Pardon Cæsar; Cæsar, pardon:	
	As low as to thy foot doth Cassius fall,	
	To beg enfranchisement for Publius Cimber	
CÆSAR	I could be well moved, if I were as you;	
	If I could pray to move, prayers would move me.	
	But I am constant as the northern star,	60
	Of whose true-fixed and resting quality	
	There is no fellow in the firmament.	
	The skies are painted with unnumbered sparks,	
	They are all fire, and every one doth shine;	
	But there's but one in all doth hold his place.	
	So in the world; 'tis furnished well with men,	
	And men are flesh and blood, and apprehensive;	
	Yet in the number I do know but one	
	That unassailable holds on his rank,	
	Unshaked of motion; and that I am he,	70
	Let me a little show it, even in this,	
	That I was constant Cimber should be banished,	
	And constant do remain to keep him so.	
CINNA	O Cæsar -	
CÆSAR	Hence! Wilt thou lift up Olympus?	
DECIUS	Great Cæsar -	
CÆSAR	Doth not Brutus bootless kneel?	
CASCA	Speak hands for me!	
	[*They stab Cæsar*	
CÆSAR	Et tu Brute? Then fall Cæsar! *Dies*	
CINNA	Liberty! Freedom! Tyranny is dead.	

Brutus assures everyone that there will be no more killing. The crowd flee. The conspirators cover their hands and weapons in Cæsar's blood.

proclaim: announce
common pulpits: public speaking places
Ambition's debt is paid: ambition has got its deserts (i.e. there is no danger to anyone else)
confounded with this mutiny: amazed by this rebellion
do your age some mischief: harm you in your old age
abide: answer for
doomsday: the Day of Judgement
Fates . . . stand upon: We would like to know what the future holds. We know we have to die, but men wonder about when it will happen and how long they have left.
Grant . . . benefit: If you believe that then death is a blessing
abridged: shortened
besmear: cover

Run hence, proclaim, cry it about the streets.

CASSIUS   Some to the common pulpits, and cry out,   80
'Liberty, freedom, and enfranchisement!'

BRUTUS   People and senators, be not affrighted.
Fly not, stand still. Ambition's debt is paid.

CASSIUS   Go to the pulpit Brutus.

DECIUS   And Cassius too.

BRUTUS   Where's Publius?

CINNA   Here, quite confounded with this mutiny.

METELLUS   Stand fast together, lest some friend of Cæsar's
Should chance -

BRUTUS   Talk not of standing. Publius, good cheer;
There is no harm intended to your person,   90
Nor to no Roman else. So tell them Publius.

CASCA   And leave us Publius, lest that the people
Rushing on us should do your age some mischief.

BRUTUS   Do so; and let no man abide this deed,
But we the doers.

Enter TREBONIUS

CASSIUS   Where is Antony?

TREBONIUS   Fled to his house amazed.
Men, wives, and children stare, cry out, and run,
As it were doomsday.

BRUTUS   Fates, we will know your pleasures.
That we shall die we know; 'tis but the time,
And drawing days out, that men stand upon.   100

CASCA   Why he that cuts off twenty years of life
Cuts off so many years of fearing death.

BRUTUS   Grant that, and then is death a benefit;
So are we Cæsar's friends, that have abridged
His time of fearing death. Stoop Romans, stoop,
And let us bathe our hands in Cæsar's blood
Up to the elbows, and besmear our swords;

Cassius says they will be remembered as heroes. Antony's servant arrives to ask if his master can come safely to hear the reasons for Cæsar's death.

lofty: high (of the highest motives)

in sport: on the stage (Shakespeare frequently refers to the theatre. Whenever the play is performed, the audience is seeing Cæsar's death 'in sport ')

Pompey's basis: the base of Pompey's statue (Cæsar was actually murdered near Pompey's Theatre; Shakespeare has moved the scene of death to the Capitol)

knot: group

prostrate: lying face downwards

vouchsafe: grant

be resolved: have it explained

hazards: dangers

untrod state: new conditions

	Then walk we forth, even to the market place,
	And waving our red weapons o'er our heads,
	Let's all cry, 'Peace, freedom, and liberty!' 110
CASSIUS	Stoop then, and wash. How many ages hence
	Shall this our lofty scene be acted over,
	In states unborn and accents yet unknown.
BRUTUS	How many times shall Cæsar bleed in sport,
	That now on Pompey's basis lies along,
	No worthier than the dust.
CASSIUS	So oft as that shall be,
	So often shall the knot of us be called
	The men that gave their country liberty.
DECIUS	What, shall we forth?
CASSIUS	Ay, every man away.
	Brutus shall lead, and we will grace his heels 120
	With the most boldest and best hearts of Rome.

Enter a SERVANT

BRUTUS	Soft, who comes here? A friend of Antony's.
SERVANT	Thus Brutus, did my master bid me kneel;
	Thus did Mark Antony bid me fall down,
	And being prostrate thus he bade me say:
	Brutus is noble, wise, valiant, and honest;
	Cæsar was mighty, bold, royal, and loving.
	Say I love Brutus, and I honour him;
	Say I feared Cæsar, honoured him, and loved
	him.
	If Brutus will vouchsafe that Antony 130
	May safely come to him, and be resolved
	How Cæsar hath deserved to lie in death,
	Mark Antony shall not love Cæsar dead
	So well as Brutus living; but will follow
	The fortunes and affairs of noble Brutus
	Through the hazards of this untrod state
	With all true faith. So says my master Antony.
BRUTUS	Thy master is a wise and valiant Roman;

Brutus reassures Antony's servant that no harm will come to Antony. Cassius again expresses misgivings. Antony arrives and says that if the conspirators are going to kill him, too, then he wants to die alongside Cæsar.

He shall be satisfied: it will be explained to his satisfaction
presently: at once
well to friend: as a good friend
my misgiving . . . purpose: my doubts still hold good
spoils: things gained from war
let blood: made to bleed
rank: overgrown, grown too big
bear me hard: have a grudge against me
purpled: (suggesting that Cæsar's blood was of royal colour would not win Antony many friends)
so apt: a better time
mean: means
cut off: cut down
The choice . . . age: the pick of this generation (Cassius would agree with him, but does Antony really mean this?)

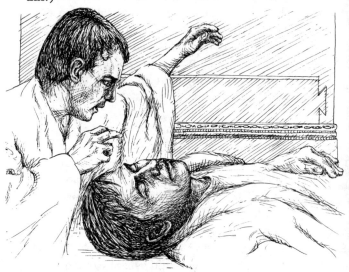

I never thought him worse.
Tell him, so please him come unto this place,   140
He shall be satisfied; and by my honour
Depart untouched.

SERVANT   I'll fetch him presently.

[*Exit*

BRUTUS   I know that we shall have him well to friend.
CASSIUS   I wish we may. But yet have I a mind
            That fears him much; and my misgiving still
            Falls shrewdly to the purpose.
BRUTUS   But here comes Antony.

Enter ANTONY

                         Welcome Mark Antony.
ANTONY   O mighty Cæsar! Dost thou lie so low?
            Are all thy conquests, glories, triumphs, spoils,
            Shrunk to this little measure? Fare thee well.   150
            I know not gentlemen what you intend,
            Who else must be let blood, who else is rank;
            If I myself, there is no hour so fit
            As Cæsar's death hour, nor no instrument
            Of half that worth as those your swords, made
              rich
            With the most noble blood of all this world.
            I do beseech ye, if you bear me hard,
            Now, whilst your purpled hands do reek and
              smoke,
            Fulfil your pleasure. Live a thousand years,
            I shall not find myself so apt to die;   160
            No place will please me so, no mean of death,
            As here by Cæsar, and by you cut off,
            The choice and master spirits of this age.
BRUTUS   O Antony, beg not your death of us.
            Though now we must appear bloody and cruel,

Brutus welcomes Antony with love, and assures him that Cæsar died for a good reason. Antony shakes hands with the conspirators.

pitiful: full of pity

And pity to . . . pity: we have strong feelings for Rome and they overcame our feelings for Cæsar

have leaden points: are blunt (and therefore will not hurt), like lead

in strength of malice: (this does not make sense. One suggestion is that, at some time, 'malice' was wrongly copied; 'welcoe' -welcome- could have been the original word)

reverence: respect

disposing of the new dignities: allocating official jobs

appeased: calmed

deliver you the cause: give you the reason

render: give

Gentlemen all: (does Antony really mean this?)

credit: credibility

conceit: think of

As by our hands and this our present act,
You see we do; yet see you but our hands,
And this the bleeding business they have done.
Our hearts you see not, they are pitiful;
And pity to the general wrong of Rome -   170
As fire drives out fire, so pity pity -
Hath done this deed on Cæsar. For your part,
To you our swords have leaden points, Mark
        Antony;
Our arms, in strength of malice, and our hearts
Of brothers' temper, do receive you in
With all kind love, good thoughts, and reverence.

CASSIUS   Your voice shall be as strong as any man's
In the disposing of new dignities.

BRUTUS   Only be patient till we have appeased
The multitude, beside themselves with fear,   180
And then we will deliver you the cause,
Why I, that did love Cæsar when I struck him,
Have thus proceeded.

ANTONY   I doubt not of your wisdom.
Let each man render me his bloody hand.
First Marcus Brutus, will I shake with you;
Next Caius Cassius, do I take your hand;
Now Decius Brutus yours; now yours Metellus;
Yours Cinna; and my valiant Casca, yours;
Though last, not least in love, yours good
        Trebonius.
Gentlemen all - alas, what shall I say?   190
My credit now stands on such slippery ground,
That one of two bad ways you must conceit me,
Either a coward or a flatterer.
That I did love thee Cæsar, O 'tis true.
If then thy spirit look upon us now,
Shall it not grieve thee dearer than thy death,
To see thy Antony making his peace,
Shaking the bloody fingers of thy foes,

Antony fears he is doing Cæsar wrong by befriending the conspirators. He praises Cæsar, but assures Cassius he can be counted on if Cæsar's death is justified.

most noble: (again, does Antony really mean this?)

corse: corpse

become me better: be more fitting

bayed: trapped

hart: deer (hart/heart, play on words, see Metaphor in the Glossary)

signed in thy spoil: signified by your blood

Lethe: a river of the underworld; here the meaning is 'life-blood'

this, indeed: (Antony gestures towards the body)

O world . . . thee: Cæsar was a hart in the world, and the heart of the world

The enemies ... this: even Cæsar's enemies would admit this

cold modesty: moderate language

compact: agreement

pricked: marked down

therefore: for that reason

wherein: in what way

or else: otherwise

suitor: one with a request

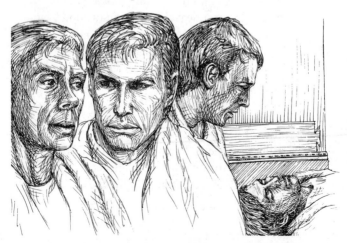

Most noble, in the presence of thy corse?
Had I as many eyes as thou hast wounds,   200
Weeping as fast as they stream forth thy blood,
It would become me better than to close
In terms of friendship with thine enemies.
Pardon me Julius! Here wast thou bayed, brave
 hart;
Here didst thou fall; and here thy hunters stand,
Signed in thy spoil, and crimsoned in thy lethe.
O world, thou wast the forest to this hart,
And this, indeed, O world, the heart of thee.
How like a deer, strucken by many princes,
Dost thou here lie.   210

CASSIUS Mark Antony -

ANTONY   Pardon me Caius Cassius,
The enemies of Cæsar shall say this;
Then, in a friend, it is cold modesty.

CASSIUS I blame you not for praising Cæsar so,
But what compact mean you to have with us?
Will you be pricked in number of our friends,
Or shall we on, and not depend on you?

ANTONY Therefore I took your hands, but was indeed
Swayed from the point by looking down on
 Cæsar.
Friends am I with you all, and love you all,   220
Upon this hope, that you shall give me reasons
Why, and wherein, Cæsar was dangerous.

BRUTUS Or else were this a savage spectacle.
Our reasons are so full of good regard,
That were you, Antony, the son of Cæsar,
You should be satisfied.

ANTONY   That's all I seek;
And am moreover suitor that I may
Produce his body to the market place,
And in the pulpit, as becomes a friend,
Speak in the order of his funeral.   230

Cassius worries that Antony is to be allowed to speak at Cæsar's funeral. Left alone with the body, Antony drops all pretence of friendship with the conspirators.

protest: declare
advantage: do us good
fall: happen
piece of earth: body (a reference to 'ashes to ashes, dust to dust')
tide of times: measurable time

BRUTUS You shall, Mark Antony.

CASSIUS Brutus, a word with you.
[*Aside to Brutus*] You know not what you do.
Do not consent
That Antony speak in his funeral.
Know you how much the people may be moved
By that which he will utter?

BRUTUS By your pardon;
I will myself into the pulpit first,
And show the reason of our Cæsar's death.
What Antony shall speak, I will protest
He speaks by leave, and by permission;
And that we are contented Cæsar shall   240
Have all true rites, and lawful ceremonies.
It shall advantage more than do us wrong.

CASSIUS I know not what may fall; I like it not.

BRUTUS Mark Antony, here take you Cæsar's body.
You shall not in your funeral speech blame us,
But speak all good you can devise of Cæsar,
And say you do't by our permission;
Else shall you not have any hand at all
About his funeral. And you shall speak
In the same pulpit whereto I am going,   250
After my speech is ended.

ANTONY Be it so;
I do desire no more.

BRUTUS Prepare the body then, and follow us.

[*Exeunt all but Antony*

ANTONY O pardon me, thou bleeding piece of earth,
That I am meek and gentle with these butchers.
Thou art the ruins of the noblest man
That ever lived in the tide of times.
Woe to the hand that shed this costly blood!
Over thy wounds now do I prophesy,
Which like dumb mouths do ope their ruby lips,   260

Antony prophesies civil war. Octavius Cæsar is coming to Rome. Antony tells Octavius' servant to wait and see how the crowd react at Cæsar's funeral, before reporting back to Octavius.

light: fall
cumber: weigh down
in use: normal
quartered: cut into quarters
custom of fell deeds: being used to savagery
ranging: wandering
Ate: (Ah-teh) Roman goddess of revenge
confines: territories
havoc: 'No mercy'
let slip the dogs of war: (metaphor of greyhounds on leashes)
carrion: dead, rotting
Octavius Cæsar: a distant relative of Julius, Octavius was to become Emperor himself. At this stage he has been favoured by Julius Cæsar because of his ability, not his family connections, and is regarded as his heir.
Passion: emotion
league: about three miles
Post: hurry
chanced: happened
Hie: go quickly
not(go)**back**
try: test

To beg the voice and utterance of my tongue,
A curse shall light upon the limbs of men;
Domestic fury, and fierce civil strife
Shall cumber all the parts of Italy;
Blood and destruction shall be so in use,
And dreadful objects so familiar,
That mothers shall but smile when they behold
Their infants quartered with the hands of war;
All pity choked with custom of fell deeds;
And Cæsar's spirit ranging for revenge,   270
With Ate by his side come hot from hell,
Shall in these confines with a monarch's voice
Cry havoc, and let slip the dogs of war,
That this foul deed shall smell above the earth
With carrion men, groaning for burial.

Enter a SERVANT

You serve Octavius Cæsar, do you not?

SERVANT   I do Mark Antony.

ANTONY   Cæsar did write for him to come to Rome.

SERVANT   He did receive his letters, and is coming,
And bid me to say to you by word of mouth -   280
O Cæsar!

ANTONY   Thy heart is big; get thee apart and weep.
Passion I see is catching, for mine eyes,
Seeing those beads of sorrow stand in thine,
Began to water. Is thy master coming?

SERVANT   He lies tonight within seven leagues of Rome.

ANTONY   Post back with speed, and tell him what hath
                chanced.
Here is a mourning Rome, a dangerous Rome,
No Rome of safety for Octavius yet;
Hie hence, and tell him so. Yet stay awhile,   290
Thou shalt not back till I have borne this corse
Into the market place. There shall I try
In my oration, how the people take

issue: handiwork
discourse: tell

Keeping track

1 Why is it important for the conspirators to get Antony out of the way?

2 What do Cæsar's last words tell us about his feelings for Brutus?

3 How is the action of lines 105-107 connected with Calphurnia?

4 Through which character does Shakespeare warn the audience that Antony could mean trouble for the conspirators?

5 What does Antony really think of the conspirators?

6 Do you think that Octavius' arrival signals good news or bad news for the conspirators? Why?

Discussion

1 Assassination is an outrageous crime, but Shakespeare shows Cæsar in such a light (lines 39-48, 58-73) that the Elizabethan audience might well feel that he gets what he asks for. What is your opinion?

2 It has been said that Antony's courage and oratory (skill in speaking) are remarkable in the circumstances. What has happened – and what is happening – which might threaten his safety and make it difficult to think clearly?

The cruel issue of these bloody men;
According to the which, thou shalt discourse
To young Octavius of the state of things.
Lend me your hand.

[*Exeunt with Cæsar's body*

Drama

Et tu Brute?

Groups of 9.

This is a tense and famous moment but it can be trivialised
and made to look ludicrous unless you remember that all the
conspirators stab Cæsar one after the other. The act of
stabbing really belongs in the back alley, but on this occasion
it is carried out in public, in fact before the senate. It is a
ritualistic act and has to be done in a stylised manner. The act
must be slowed down and performed as a ceremony. In Act 2
scene 1 Brutus says 'Let's carve him as a dish fit for gods, Not
hew him as a carcass fit for hounds.' and '… we shall be called
purgers not murderers.'

1 Plan a slow motion version of the stabbing of Cæsar (see
   Forum theatre, p 244).
2 You need to decide the order of strike between Casca and
   Brutus.
3 Think about these points:
   ● Many of the conspirators are kneeling to start with.
   ● Why does he not fall?
   ● Are the conspirators' blows firm or tentative?
   ● Each conspirator will stab Cæsar differently with more
     or less hatred, courage or temerity, bravado or seriousness.

- Remember that this is a ceremony. Slow the blows down.
- Find a suitable sound effect to accompany the stabs. What sounds does Cæsar make at each blow?
- Does Cæsar make eye contact with each conspirator – perhaps speaks their names?
- Are some of the blows from behind?
- Are they downward, upward or straight thrusts?
- The smearing of hands with his blood is part of the ceremony – how is this done?

4 Practise your version of the assassination.

5 When you are ready, share it with the rest of the class.

Character

1 Casca has been chosen, or has volunteered, to strike the first blow (lines 19/76). What sort of person would be needed to do this? Is Casca the best man for the job?

2 In Act 1 scene 2 Cassius called Antony 'a shrewd contriver' whilst Brutus said 'he can do no more than Cæsar's arm when Cæsar's head is off'. At this stage, who seems to know Antony better? Why?

3 Bring up to date your Character logs on Brutus, Cassius, Cæsar, Casca and Antony.

Close study

1 Some modern plays have many stage directions ('moves to door', 'picks up newspaper'). Shakespeare usually only indicates entrances and exits, and actors have to work out their movements from the words of the text. What stage directions would you give for the following lines of this scene: 4-5, 6-7, 10, 55–57, 74, 76, 82–83, 123–124, 148, 151.

2 After the assassination, Antony sends his servant to speak to Brutus. Why do you think Brutus was chosen? Why does Antony not appear himself at this stage?

Writing

Artemidorus and the Soothsayer meet, fleeing from the
Capitol after Cæsar's death. They talk about the
assassination, and how it could have been avoided, if only...
They might also guess at what the future holds, although for
one of them it could be more than just guesswork. In script
form, write their conversation.

Quiz

Who said the following, and to whom?
1 'Speak hands for me'
2 'To you our swords have leaden points'
3 'Friends am I with you all, and love you all'

Who said the following about whom?
4 'Thy master is a wise and valiant Roman'
5 'But yet have I a mind
   That fears him much'
6 'the ruins of the noblest man
   That ever lived in the tide of times'

Do you remember?
7 Whose comment frightened Cassius?
8 Who pleaded for his brother's re-instatement?
9 Where Antony was when Cæsar was killed?
10 Who is coming to Rome at Cæsar's request?

Brutus speaks to the people. Cassius takes some of the crowd elsewhere to address them.

We . . . satisfied: give us information
part: divide
severally: separately
last: end
lovers: friends
Believe me . . . may believe: repetition as the crowd
    settles to silence
censure: judge

SCENE 2

The Forum.
Enter BRUTUS *and* CASSIUS, *and Citizens*

CITIZENS   We will be satisfied; let us be satisfied.

BRUTUS   Then follow me, and give me audience, friends.
             Cassius, go you into the other street,
             And part the numbers.
             Those that will hear me speak, let 'em stay here;
             Those that will follow Cassius, go with him;
             And public reasons shall be rendered   10
             Of Cæsar's death.

1ST CITIZEN   I will hear Brutus speak.

2ND CITIZEN I will hear Cassius, and compare their reasons,
             When severally we hear them rendered

                    [*Exit Cassius, with some of the Citizens.*
                        Brutus goes into the pulpit

3RD CITIZEN The noble Brutus is ascended. Silence!

BRUTUS   Be patient till the last.
             Romans, countrymen, and lovers, hear me for my
             cause, and be silent, that you may hear. Believe
             me for mine honour, and have respect to mine
             honour, that you may believe.
             Censure me in your wisdom, and awake your
             senses, that you may the better judge. If there be
             any in this assembly, any dear friend of Cæsar's,
             to him I say, that Brutus' love to Cæsar was no
             less than his. If then that friend demand why

The crowd approve of Brutus' speech. They cheer him enthusiastically.

so base: so low
bondman: slave
rude: rough
question: case
enrolled: officially documented
extenuated: lessened
enforced: exaggerated
commonwealth: welfare of everyone
lover: friend

Brutus rose against Cæsar, this is my answer -
not that I loved Cæsar less, but that I loved
Rome more. Had you rather Caesar were living,
and die all slaves, than that Cæsar were dead, to
live all free men? As Cæsar loved me, I weep for
him; as he was fortunate, I rejoice at it; as he was
valiant, I honour him; but as he was ambitious, I
slew him. There is tears, for his love; joy, for his
fortune; honour, for his valour; and death, for his
ambition. Who is here so base, that would be a
bondman? If any, speak, for him have I offended.
Who is here so rude that would not be a Roman? If
any, speak, for him have I offended. Who is here so
vile that will not love his country? If any, speak, for
him have I offended. I pause for a reply.   36

ALL   None Brutus, none.

BRUTUS   Then none have I offended. I have done no
             more to Cæsar than you shall do to Brutus. The
             question of his death is enrolled in the Capitol;
             his glory not extenuated, wherein he was
             worthy; nor his offences enforced, for which he
             suffered death.

             Enter ANTONY *with* CÆSAR'S *body*

             Here comes his body, mourned by Mark
             Antony, who though he had no hand in his
             death, shall receive the benefit of his dying, a
             place in the commonwealth, as which of you
             shall not? With this I depart, that as I slew my
             best lover for the good of Rome, I have the same
             dagger for myself, when it shall please my
             country to need my death.   51

ALL   Live Brutus, live, live!

1ST CITIZEN Bring him with triumph home unto his house.

2ND CITIZEN Give him a statue with his ancestors.

3RD CITIZEN Let him be Cæsar.

Brutus urges the crowd to stay and listen to what Antony has to say.

parts: qualities
entreat: beg
Do grace: honour
beholding: obliged

4TH CITIZEN	Cæsar's better parts
	Shall be crowned in Brutus.
1ST CITIZEN	We'll bring him to his house with shouts and
	clamours.
BRUTUS	My countrymen -
2ND CITIZEN	Peace, silence, Brutus speaks.
1ST CITIZEN	Peace ho!
BRUTUS	Good countrymen, let me depart alone.

60

And, for my sake, stay here with Antony.
Do grace to Cæsar's corpse, and grace his
    speech
Tending to Cæsar's glories, which Mark
    Antony,
By our permission, is allowed to make.
I do entreat you, not a man depart,
Save I alone, till Antony have spoke.

[*Exit*

1ST CITIZEN	Stay ho, and let us hear Mark Antony.
3RD CITIZEN	Let him go up into the public chair.
	We'll hear him. Noble Antony go up.

70

ANTONY	For Brutus' sake, I am beholding to you.

[*Goes into the pulpit*

4TH CITIZEN	What does he say of Brutus?
3RD CITIZEN	He says, for Brutus' sake
	He finds himself beholding to us all.
4TH CITIZEN	'Twere best he speak no harm of Brutus here.
1ST CITIZEN	This Cæsar was a tyrant.
3RD CITIZEN	Nay that's certain.
	We are blest that Rome is rid of him.
2ND CITIZEN	Peace, let us hear what Antony can say.
ANTONY	You gentle Romans -
CITIZEN	Peace ho, let us hear him.

Antony appears to be agreeing with Brutus'
assessment of Cæsar, but Brutus' insistence that
Antony should not condemn the conspirators is back-
firing.

---

interred: buried
under leave of: by permission of
Brutus is an honourable man: a) does he mean it? b)
    how often is this phrase repeated in his speech?
just: fair
general coffers: public funds
sterner: stronger
thrice: three times
brutish beasts: animals (Antony must feel that the crowd
    is now on his side. He would not have opened his speech
    this way.)

ANTONY   Friends, Romans, countrymen, lend me your
                  ears:
          I come to bury Cæsar, not to praise him.
          The evil that men do lives after them,   80
          The good is oft interred with their bones;
          So let it be with Cæsar. The noble Brutus
          Hath told you Cæsar was ambitious;
          If it were so, it was a grievous fault,
          And grievously hath Cæsar answered it.
          Here, under leave of Brutus and the rest -
          For Brutus is an honourable man,
          So are they all, all honourable men -
          Come I to speak in Cæsar's funeral.
          He was my friend, faithful and just to me;   90
          But Brutus says he was ambitious,
          And Brutus is an honourable man.
          He hath brought many captives home to Rome,
          Whose ransoms did the general coffers fill.
          Did this in Cæsar seem ambitious?
          When that the poor have cried, Cæsar hath
                  wept;
          Ambition should be made of sterner stuff;
          Yet Brutus says he was ambitious,
          And Brutus is an honourable man.
          You all did see that on the Lupercal   100
          I thrice presented him a kingly crown,
          Which he did thrice refuse. Was this ambition?
          Yet Brutus says he was ambitious,
          And sure he is an honourable man.
          I speak not to disprove what Brutus spoke,
          But here I am to speak what I do know.
          You all did love him once, not without cause;
          What cause withholds you then to mourn for
                  him?
          O judgement, thou art fled to brutish beasts,
          And men have lost their reason. Bear with me; 110
          My heart is in the coffin there with Cæsar,

The crowd are now sympathetic to Antony. He reveals that he has Cæsar's will, but he cannot let them know how generous Cæsar has been to them.

I must pause: (Antony is overcome with grief)
Cæsar has had great wrong (done to him)
abide: pay for
mark: pay attention to
none so poor: he has only one mourner (Antony)
masters: (an unusual, but deliberate, form of address)
if I were disposed . . . rage: (if he did not want to stir them up, why mention it?)
parchment: document
closet: room
commons: citizens/ordinary people
testament: will
napkins: handkerchiefs
Bequeathing: leaving in a will
issue: children
And they would ... issue: (see Act 2 scene 2, 83–90)

	And I must pause till it come back to me.
1ST CITIZEN	Methinks there is much reason in his sayings.
2ND CITIZEN	If thou consider rightly of the matter,
	Cæsar has had great wrong.
3RD CITIZEN	Has he masters?
	I fear there will a worse come in his place.
4TH CITIZEN	Marked ye his words? He would not take the crown;
	Therefore 'tis certain he was not ambitious.
1ST CITIZEN	If it be found so, some will dear abide it.
2ND CITIZEN	Poor soul, his eyes are red as fire with weeping.
3RD CITIZEN	There's not a nobler man in Rome than Antony.
4TH CITIZEN	Now mark him, he begins again to speak,
ANTONY	But yesterday the word of Cæsar might

120

Have stood against the world; now lies he there,
And none so poor to do him reverence.
O masters, if I were disposed to stir
Your hearts and minds to mutiny and rage,
I should do Brutus wrong, and Cassius wrong,
Who you all know are honourable men.
I will not do them wrong; I rather choose   130
To wrong the dead, to wrong myself and you,
Than I will wrong such honourable men.
But here's a parchment with the seal of Cæsar;
I found it in his closet; 'tis his will.
Let but the commons hear this testament -
Which, pardon me, I do not mean to read -
And they would go and kiss dead Cæsar's wounds,
And dip their napkins in his sacred blood,
Yea, beg a hair of him for memory,
And dying, mention it within their wills,   140
Bequeathing it as a rich legacy
Unto their issue.

4TH CITIZEN	We'll hear the will. Read it Mark Antony.

The crowd insist on knowing the contents of the will.
Antony comes down from the pulpit and stands by
Cæsar's body.

---

you are not . . . men: does this remind you of Act 1
    scene 1?
inflame: anger
heirs: people who inherit
I have o'ershot myself: I have said too much
descend: come down from the pulpit
hearse: carriage for the body

ALL	The will, the will! We will hear Cæsar's will.
ANTONY	Have patience gentle friends, I must not read it.
	It is not meet you know how Cæsar loved you.
	You are not wood, you are not stones, but men;
	And being men, hearing the will of Cæsar,
	It will inflame you, it will make you mad.
	'Tis good you know not that you are his heirs; 150
	For if you should, O what would come of it!
4TH CITIZEN	Read the will. We'll hear it Antony.
	You shall read us the will, Cæsar's will.
ANTONY	Will you be patient? Will you stay awhile?
	I have o'ershot myself to tell you of it.
	I fear I wrong the honourable men
	Whose daggers have stabbed Cæsar; I do fear it.
4TH CITIZEN	They were traitors. Honourable men!
ALL	The will! The testament!
2ND CITIZEN	They were villains, murderers. The will, read 160 the will.
ANTONY	You will compel me then to read the will?
	Then make a ring about the corpse of Cæsar,
	And let me show you him that made the will.
	Shall I descend? And will you give me leave?
ALL	Come down.
2ND CITIZEN	Descend.
3RD CITIZEN	You shall have leave.

[Antony comes down

4TH CITIZEN	A ring, stand round.
1ST CITIZEN	Stand from the hearse, stand from the body. 170
2ND CITIZEN	Room for Antony, most noble Antony.
ANTONY	Nay, press not so upon me; bear back.
SEVERAL CITIZENS	Stand back; room; bear back.
ANTONY	If you have tears, prepare to shed them now.

Antony first shows the crowd Cæsar's clothing torn and bloodied. He then reveals the body of Cæsar to the crowd.

mantle: cloak

Nervii: Belgian tribe whom Cæsar defeated against the odds

rent: tear

envious: (the first direct criticism of the conspirators – there are more to come)

be resolved: make certain

Cæsar's angel: highly regarded by Cæsar

most unkindest: in modern speech this use of two superlatives 'most' and 'unkindest' would be considered ungrammatical. In Shakespeare's time it could be used for extra emphasis.

Ingratitude … vanquished him: it was the ingratitude of Brutus that really defeated him; it was stronger than the weapons wielded by a traitor.

fell down: suffered

dint of pity: touch of compassion

gracious drops: tears which show humanity

what weep … wounded: do you weep just at the sight of the damage done to Cæsar's clothing?

look you here: (he reveals the body)

marred . . . traitors: disfigured as traitors are

You all do know this mantle. I remember
The first time ever Cæsar put it on;
'Twas on a summer's evening in his tent,
That day he overcame the Nervii.
Look, in this place ran Cassius' dagger through.
See what a rent the envious Casca made.   180
Through this the well-beloved Brutus stabbed;
And as he plucked his cursed steel away,
Mark how the blood of Cæsar followed it,
As rushing out of doors, to be resolved
If Brutus so unkindly knocked or no;
For Brutus, as you know, was Cæsar's angel.
Judge, O you gods, how dearly Cæsar loved him.
This was the most unkindest cut of all;
For when the noble Cæsar saw him stab,
Ingratitude, more strong than traitors' arms,   190
Quite vanquished him. Then burst his mighty
    heart;
And in his mantle muffling up his face,
Even at the base of Pompey's statue,
Which all the while ran blood, great Cæsar fell.
O what a fall was there, my countrymen!
Then I, and you, and all of us fell down,
Whilst bloody treason flourished over us.
O now you weep, and I perceive you feel
The dint of pity. These are gracious drops.
Kind souls, what weep you when you but behold   200
Our Cæsar's vesture wounded? Look you here,
Here is himself, marred as you see with traitors.

1ST CITIZEN O piteous spectacle!

2ND CITIZEN O noble Cæsar!

3RD CITIZEN O woeful day!

4TH CITIZEN O traitors, villains!

1ST CITIZEN O most bloody sight!

2ND CITIZEN We will be revenged.

ALL   Revenge! About! Seek! Burn! Fire! Kill! Slay!

Antony urges the crowd to calm down. He claims to be a plain-speaking man, and says that if he could talk persuasively then they would rise to mutiny.

let me not stir you up: (this is a final calming of the crowd before he sets them loose)
private griefs: personal reasons
right on: straight
ruffle: stir
mutiny: (repetition of this word)

| | Let not a traitor live! | 210 |

ANTONY   Stay countrymen.

1ST CITIZEN Peace there, hear the noble Antony.

2ND CITIZEN We'll hear him, we'll follow him, we'll die with
              him.

ANTONY   Good friends, sweet friends, let me not stir you
              up
           To such a sudden flood of mutiny.
           They that have done this deed are honourable.
           What private griefs they have, alas, I know not,
           That made them do it. They are wise and
              honourable,
           And will no doubt with reasons answer you.   220
           I come not friends, to steal away your hearts;
           I am no orator as Brutus is;
           But as you know me all, a plain blunt man,
           That love my friend; and that they know full well
           That gave me public leave to speak of him.
           For I have neither wit, nor words, nor worth,
           Action, nor utterance, nor the power of speech,
           To stir men's blood; I only speak right on.
           I tell you that which you yourselves do know,
           Show you sweet Cæsar's wounds, poor poor
              dumb mouths,   230
           And I bid them speak for me. But were I Brutus,
           And Brutus Antony, there were an Antony
           Would ruffle up your spirits, and put a tongue
           In every wound of Cæsar that shou'd move
           The stones of Rome to rise and mutiny.

ALL   We'll mutiny.

1ST CITIZEN We'll burn the house of Brutus.

3RD CITIZEN Away then, come, seek the conspirators.

ANTONY   Yet hear me countrymen, yet hear me speak.

ALL   Peace ho, hear Antony, most noble Antony.   240

ANTONY   Why friends, you go to do you know not what.

**Cæsar has been generous in his will. The crowd leaves
to cremate Cæsar and take vengeance on the
conspirators.**

several: separate
seventy-five drachmas: at today's value, 24 pence. This,
    of course, bears no relation to their value in Roman
    times.
walks: lawns
arbours: cultivated gardens
common pleasures: public parks
recreate yourselves: enjoy yourselves at leisure
burn his body: cremate him
brands: torches
forms: seats
afoot: in action

	Wherein hath Cæsar thus deserved your loves?
	Alas you know not. I must tell you then.
	You have forgot the will I told you of.
ALL	Most true. The will, let's stay and hear the will.
ANTONY	Here is the will, and under Cæsar's seal.
	To every Roman citizen he gives,
	To every several man, seventy-five drachmas.
2ND CITIZEN	Most noble Cæsar! We'll revenge his death.
3RD CITIZEN	O royal Cæsar!	250
ANTONY	Hear me with patience.
ALL	Peace ho!
ANTONY	Moreover, he hath left you all his walks,
	His private arbours and new-planted orchards,
	On this side Tiber; he hath left them you,
	And to your heirs for ever - common pleasures,
	To walk abroad, and recreate yourselves.
	Here was a Cæsar! When comes such another?
1ST CITIZEN	Never, never. Come, away, away!
	We'll burn his body in the holy place,	260
	And with the brands fire the traitors' houses.
	Take up the body.
2ND CITIZEN	Go fetch fire.
3RD CITIZEN	Pluck down benches.
4TH CITIZEN	Pluck down forms, windows, any thing.

[*Exeunt Citizens with the body*

| ANTONY | Now let it work. Mischief, thou art afoot, |
| | Take thou what course thou wilt. |

Enter a SERVANT

How now fellow!

SERVANT	Sir, Octavius is already come to Rome.
ANTONY	Where is he?
SERVANT	He and Lepidus are at Cæsar's house.	270

Antony leaves to visit Octavius. Brutus and Cassius have already fled from Rome.

upon a wish: in response to my unspoken wish
Fortune is merry: fate is on our side
Are rid: have ridden
belike . . . notice: perhaps they heard something

In their anger, the crowd meet Cinna, the poet. They question him.

things unluckily . . . fantasy: my mind is full of bad
    omens
wander forth: go outdoors
bear me a bang: get a smack from me

ANTONY	And thither will I straight to visit him.
	He comes upon a wish. Fortune is merry,
	And in this mood will give us anything.
SERVANT	I heard him say, Brutus and Cassius
	Are rid like madmen through the gates of Rome.
ANTONY	Belike they had some notice of the people,
	How I had moved them. Bring me to Octavius.

[Exeunt

SCENE 3

Rome. A street.
Enter CINNA *the poet, and after him Citizens*

CINNA	I dreamt tonight that I did feast with Cæsar,
	And things unluckily charge my fantasy.
	I have no will to wander forth of doors,
	Yet something leads me forth.
1ST CITIZEN	What is your name?
2ND CITIZEN	Whither are you going?
3RD CITIZEN	Where do you dwell?
4TH CITIZEN	Are you a married man or a bachelor?
1ST CITIZEN	Ay, and briefly.
2ND CITIZEN	Answer every man directly
4TH CITIZEN	Ay, and wisely.
3RD CITIZEN	Ay, and truly, you were best.
CINNA	What is my name? Whither am I going? Where
	do I dwell? Am I a married man or a bachelor?
	Then to answer every man directly and briefly,
	wisely and truly - wisely I say, I am a bachelor.
2ND CITIZEN	That's as much as to say, they are fools that
	marry. You'll bear me a bang for that I fear.
	Proceed directly.
CINNA	Directly I am going to Cæsar's funeral.

10

When they learn that the poet has the same name as one of the conspirators, they drag him away to murder him.

ACTIVITIES

Keeping track

1 What reason does Brutus give the crowd for Cæsar's murder?
2 How will Brutus be feeling as he leaves the market place?
3 How does Antony answer Brutus' criticism of Cæsar (see question 1)?
4 Is Antony's mention of the will really accidental, or has he other motives?
5 Antony was not there when Cæsar died. Why, then, does he claim to know who delivered which blow?

1ST CITIZEN	As a friend or an enemy?
CINNA	As a friend.
2ND CITIZEN	That matter is answered directly.
4TH CITIZEN	For your dwelling - briefly.
CINNA	Briefly, I dwell by the Capitol.
3RD CITIZEN	Your name sir, truly.
CINNA	Truly, my name is Cinna.
1ST CITIZEN	Tear him to pieces, he's a conspirator.
CINNA	I am Cinna the poet, I am Cinna the poet.
4TH CITIZEN	Tear him for his bad verses, tear him for his bad verses.
CINNA	I am not Cinna the conspirator.
4TH CITIZEN	It is no matter, his name's Cinna; pluck but his name out of his heart, and turn him going.
3RD CITIZEN	Tear him, tear him! Come, brands, ho! Fire brands. To Brutus', to Cassius'; burn all. Some to Decius' house, and some to Casca's; some to Ligarius'. Away, go!

30

[*Exeunt*

6 The 1st citizen says, 'We'll burn the house of Brutus.' What did he say earlier when Brutus had finished speaking (p135)?

Discussion

1 How do you think Brutus and Cassius 'had some notice of the people', giving them time to escape?
2 Act 3 scene 3 shows the ugly mood of the mob, but it has been said that there is also a little comic relief before the savage finale. Suggest why this scene is structured like this.

3 What are the problems of staging Act 3 scene 3? (Look at the numbers involved, the speed of action and the pitch of voices.) Why does the murder of Cinna not take place on stage?

4 Things have obviously gone very wrong for the conspirators. What mistakes have they made which have led to the dangerous situation in which they now find themselves? Is any one person particularly to blame?

Drama

Groups of three ('A', 'B', and 'C').

1 Look carefully at Brutus and Antony's speeches.

2 Decide who will be A, B or C. They are all plebeians:
A heard both speeches and thinks Brutus' argument was best.
B heard both speeches and is for Mark Antony.
C did not hear either speech and desperately wants to know:
- what is going on
- what the two speakers said
- what to do next.

3 Begin with A and B arguing. B is wanting to go and burn Brutus' house. A is trying to prevent him. C arrives. A and B try to persuade C of the rightness of their point of view.

4 Swap roles.

Character

1 'Now let it work. Mischief, thou art afoot,
Take what course thou wilt!'
Antony has stirred the crowd to a frenzy. Can he foresee the sort of things the mob might do? Do you think he is really concerned about what is going to happen? What are his motives?

2 From the behaviour of the 4th citizen in Scenes 2 and 3, what can you say about him?

3 Your Character log on Casca can now be closed. Bring up to date your logs on Brutus, Cassius, Cæsar and Antony.

Close study

1 Antony's 'Friends, Romans, countrymen' is very similar to Brutus' 'Romans, countrymen and lovers'. But now that you have looked at both speeches, can you say why each man chose to begin with that particular order of words?

2 Brutus appeals to the reason of the crowd. Pick out some examples of balanced sentences, similar to those on page 77.

3 On the other hand, Antony appeals to the emotions of the crowd:
'When that the poor have cried, Cæsar hath wept'
'You all did love him once, not without cause'
'It is not meet you know how Cæsar loved you'.
Towards the end of his description of Cæsar's murder, lines 174–202, we know that he has been successful in winning over the crowd. Which line-and-a-half tells us this?

4 Why is Antony more successful than Brutus? Is it because he speaks last? Has he a better case to argue? Does he have a better understanding of the people? Is he a better speaker?

5 In questions 2 and 3 above, you looked at the content of the two speeches, and the delivery (the way in which they were spoken). Does that explain why one speech is in prose and the other in verse? If someone said Brutus was 'doing a Casca', referring to Act 1 scene 2, what do you think that would mean?

Development

1 When Brutus finishes speaking he is happy to leave and allow Antony to address the crowd. Why is this? What would his thoughts be at the time?

2 Antony sees the reactions of the crowd to Brutus' speech. What do you think is going through his mind as he prepares to speak?

3 If Brutus had decided to stay and listen to Antony. At what point would he have interrupted, do you think? What could he have said? What would have been the crowd's response?

Writing

1 Imagine you were in charge of Cæsar's security on the ides of March. Write a short report on the assassination for your senior officer, explaining how the conspirators were able to get so close to Cæsar without arousing suspicion.

2 Casca, the First to Strike.

Write two paragraphs about Casca.

- In the first paragraph say what a casual observer of Act 1 might have thought about Casca (e.g. dull, superstitious).

- In the second paragraph say what qualities Casca has which led the others to choose him to strike the first blow at Cæsar (e.g. courage, reliability). Your Character log will help you with this writing.

Quiz

Who said the following, and to whom?

1 'Romans, countrymen and lovers'

2 'Friends, Romans, countrymen'

3 'What is my name? Whither am I going? Where do I dwell?'

Who said the following about whom?

4 'As he was ambitious I slew him'

5 'He was my friend, faithful and just to me'

6 'I fear there will a worse come in his place'

When were the following said, and by whom?

7 (a) 'We are blest that Rome is rid of him'
   (b) 'Most noble Cæsar, we'll revenge his death'
8 (a) ''Twere best he speak no harm of Brutus here'
   (b) 'We'll burn the house of Brutus'
9 (a) 'So are they all, all honourable men'
   (b) 'They were traitors. Honourable men!'
10 (a) 'Live, Brutus, live, live!'
   (b) 'There's not a nobler man in Rome than Antony'

Antony, Octavius and Lepidus have become a triumvirate, a group of three leaders each with equal power. They have a death-list which includes some of their own relatives. Antony is unimpressed by Lepidus.

pricked: marked
damn: condemn
cut off ... legacies: Cæsar's money will pay for some of our expenses
Or ... or: Either ... or
slight unmeritable: insignificant, worthless
meet: suitable
So you thought ... proscription: That is what you thought when you agreed with him about who should be sentenced to death.
proscription: penalty of death
to ease ... loads: to share the burden of all the accusations that will be thrown at us
divers: various

Act four

Rome. A room in Antony's house.
ANTONY, OCTAVIUS, *and* LEPIDUS, *seated at a table*

ANTONY	These many then shall die; their names are pricked.
OCTAVIUS	Your brother too must die; consent you Lepidus?
LEPIDUS	I do consent -
OCTAVIUS	Prick him down Antony.
LEPIDUS	Upon condition Publius shall not live,
	Who is your sister's son, Mark Antony.
ANTONY	He shall not live; look, with a spot I damn him.
	But Lepidus, go you to Cæsar's house;
	Fetch the will hither, and we shall determine
	How to cut off some charge in legacies.
LEPIDUS	What, shall I find you here? 10
OCTAVIUS	Or here, or at the Capitol.

[Exit Lepidus

ANTONY	This is a slight unmeritable man,
	Meet to be sent on errands. Is it fit,
	The three-fold world divided, he should stand
	One of the three to share it?
OCTAVIUS	So you thought him,
	And took his voice who should be pricked to die,
	In our black sentence and proscription.
ANTONY	Octavius, I have seen more days than you;
	And though we lay these honours on this man,
	To ease ourselves of divers sland'rous loads, 20
	He shall but bear them as the ass bears gold,

Antony says they must prepare for war against Brutus and Cassius.

---

turn him off: put him out to grass
provender: fodder
wind: turn
corporal: bodily
barren-spirited: mean-minded, lacking in ideas
one that feeds … fashion: a difficult passage. It probably means he picks up ideas only after they are out of fashion with everyone else.
property: piece of furniture
levying powers: raising forces
our means stretched: our resources used fully
covert matters … disclosed: secret dangers may be revealed
answered: dealt with
at the stake … about: a reference to bear-baiting, where the bear was tied to a stake in the middle of the arena and held at bay by dogs which were set on it.

To groan and sweat under the business,
Either led or driven, as we point the way;
And having brought our treasure where we will,
Then take we down his load, and turn him off,
Like to the empty ass, to shake his ears,
And graze in commons.

OCTAVIUS   You may do your will;
But he's a tried and valiant soldier.

ANTONY   So is my horse Octavius, and for that
I do appoint him store of provender.   30
It is a creature that I teach to fight,
To wind, to stop, to run directly on,
His corporal motion governed by my spirit.
And, in some taste, is Lepidus but so;
He must be taught, and trained, and bid go forth.
A barren-spirited fellow; one that feeds
On objects, arts, and imitations,
Which, out of use and staled by other men,
Begin his fashion. Do not talk of him
But as a property. And now Octavius,   40
Listen great things. Brutus and Cassius
Are levying powers; we must straight make head.
Therefore let our alliance be combined,
Our best friends made, our means stretched;
And let us presently go sit in council,
How covert matters may be best disclosed,
And open perils surest answered.

OCTAVIUS   Let us do so; for we are at the stake,
And bayed about with many enemies;
And some that smile have in their hearts, I fear,   50
Millions of mischiefs.

                                                        [*Exeunt*

Brutus and Cassius are to meet after a long interval. Lucilius reports that Cassius has changed.

salutation: greeting
change (of attitude)
satisfied: informed to my satisfaction
resolved: easy in my mind
enforced: exaggerated
hot at hand: ready to be off
mettle: spirit

SCENE **2**

Before Brutus' tent near Sardis.
Drum. Enter BRUTUS, LUCILIUS, LUCIUS, *and*
Soldiers, TITINIUS *and* PINDARUS *meet them*

BRUTUS	Stand ho!
LUCILIUS	Give the word ho! and stand.
BRUTUS	What now Lucilius, is Cassius near?
LUCILIUS	He is at hand, and Pindarus is come To do you salutation from his master.
BRUTUS	He greets me well. Your master, Pindarus, In his own change, or by ill officers, Hath given me some worthy cause to wish Things done, undone. But if he be at hand, I shall be satisfied.
PINDARUS	I do not doubt But that my noble master will appear Such as he is, full of regard and honour.
BRUTUS	He is not doubted. A word Lucilius; How he received you, let me be resolved.
LUCILIUS	With courtesy, and with respect enough, But not with such familiar instances, Nor with such free and friendly conference, As he hath used of old.
BRUTUS	Thou hast described A hot friend cooling. Ever note Lucilius, When love begins to sicken and decay It useth an enforced ceremony. There are no tricks in plain and simple faith; But hollow men, like horses hot at hand, Make gallant show and promise of their mettle;

10

20

[Low march within

Cassius arrives and begins to argue. Brutus suggests that their discussion should be in private.

crests: arched necks
jades: poor horses
sink: fail
horse: cavalry
Wrong I mine enemies?: (It was Brutus' plan to release prisoners without ransom and so win their hearts)
sober: innocent
softly: quietly
wrangle: argue
enlarge: go into detail
charges: troops

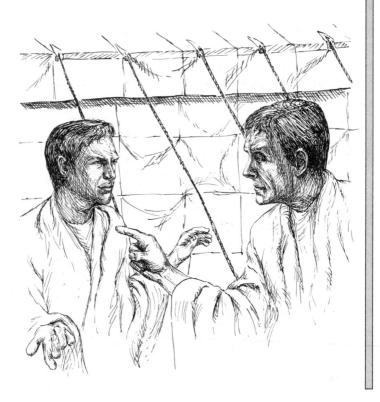

But when they should endure the bloody spur,
They fall their crests, and like deceitful jades
Sink in the trial. Comes his army on?

LUCILIUS They mean this night in Sardis to be quartered.
The greater part, the horse in general,
Are come with Cassius.

BRUTUS   Hark, he is arrived.   30
March gently on to meet him.

Enter CASSIUS *and his Powers*

CASSIUS Stand ho!

BRUTUS Stand ho! Speak the word along.

1ST SOLDIER Stand!

2ND SOLDIER Stand!

3RD SOLDIER Stand!

CASSIUS Most noble brother, you have done me wrong.

BRUTUS Judge me you gods; wrong I mine enemies?
And if not so, how should I wrong a brother?

CASSIUS Brutus, this sober form of yours hides wrongs,   40
And when you do them -

BRUTUS   Cassius, be content,
Speak your griefs softly, I do know you well.
Before the eyes of both our armies here,
Which should perceive nothing but love from us,
Let us not wrangle. Bid them move away.
Then in my tent Cassius, enlarge your griefs.
And I will give you audience.

CASSIUS   Pindarus,
Bid our commanders lead their charges off
A little from this ground.

BRUTUS Lucius, do you the like; and let no man   50
Come to our tent till we have done our
    conference.
Lucilius and Titinius guard our door.

[*Exeunt*

Brutus accuses Cassius of corruption. Cassius says he would have killed anyone else making such an accusation. Brutus reminds Cassius that Cæsar died in the name of justice.

condemned and noted: accused and branded
praying on his side: speaking on his behalf
slighted off: ignored
case: cause
meet: fitting
nice: trivial
bear his comment: be criticised
have an itching palm: be ready to take bribes
mart: market
chastisement: punishment
Contaminate: dirty
sell ... honours: profit from our position by selling jobs, offices
be a dog ... moon: be a nervous (ineffective) watchdog

SCENE 3

Within Brutus' tent.
BRUTUS *and* CASSIUS *enter the tent*

CASSIUS   That you have wronged me doth appear in this:
You have condemned and noted Lucius Pella
For taking bribes here of the Sardians;
Wherein my letters, praying on his side,
Because I knew the man, were slighted off.

BRUTUS   You wronged yourself to write in such a case.

CASSIUS   In such a time as this it is not meet
That every nice offence should bear his comment.

BRUTUS   Let me tell you Cassius, you yourself
Are much condemned to have an itching palm, 10
To sell and mart your offices for gold
To underservers.

CASSIUS   I an itching palm!
You know that you are Brutus that speak this,
Or by the gods, this speech were else your last.

BRUTUS   The name of Cassius honours this corruption,
And chastisement doth therefore hide his head.

CASSIUS   Chastisement?

BRUTUS   Remember March, the ides of March remember.
Did not great Julius bleed for justice' sake?
What villain touched his body, that did stab, 20
And not for justice? What, shall one of us,
That struck the foremost man of all this world
But for supporting robbers, shall we now
Contaminate our fingers with base bribes,
And sell the mighty space of our large honours
For so much trash as may be grasped thus?
I had rather be a dog, and bay the moon,
Than such a Roman.

Brutus mocks Cassius' temper and ignores his threats.

bait not me ... hedge me in: (bear-baiting metaphor)
To make conditions: to deal with these matters
Have mind ... health: if you value your life
slight: insignificant
rash choler: quick temper
testy: irritable
digest ... spleen: control your temper, keep it down
waspish: ill-tempered
vaunting: boasting

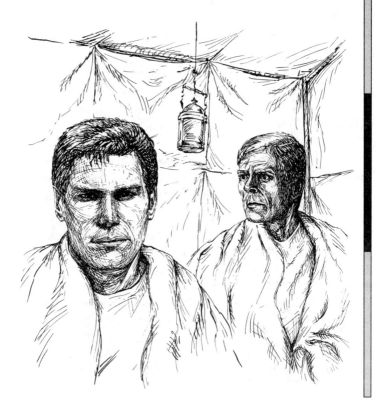

CASSIUS   Brutus, bait not me,
I'll not endure it. You forget yourself,
To hedge me in. I am a soldier, I,   30
Older in practice, abler than yourself
To make conditions.

BRUTUS   Go to! You are not, Cassius.

CASSIUS   I am.

BRUTUS   I say you are not.

CASSIUS   Urge me no more, I shall forget myself;
Have mind upon your health; tempt me no
     farther.

BRUTUS   Away slight man.

CASSIUS   Is't possible?

BRUTUS   Hear me, for I will speak.
Must I give way and room to your rash choler?
Shall I be frighted when a madman stares?   40

CASSIUS   O ye gods, ye gods! must I endure all this?

BRUTUS   All this? Ay, more. Fret till your proud heart
     break.
Go show your slaves how choleric you are,
And make bondmen tremble. Must I budge?
Must I observe you? Must I stand and crouch
Under your testy humour? By the gods,
You shall digest the venom of your spleen,
Though it do split you. For from this day forth,
I'll use you for my mirth, yea for my laughter,
When you are waspish.

CASSIUS   Is it come to this?   50

BRUTUS   You say you are a better soldier.
Let it appear so; make your vaunting true,
And it shall please me well. For mine own part,
I shall be glad to learn of noble men.

CASSIUS   You wrong me every way; you wrong me Brutus.
I said, an elder soldier, not a better.
Did I say better?

Brutus complains that Cassius refused to send him gold to pay his army.

durst: dared

presume upon: take for granted

respect not: take no notice of

denied: refused

vile: underhand, criminal

vile trash: i.e. it is vile trash when Cassius gets it; not when the peasants have it

indirection: crooked methods

coin my heart: turn my own heart into money (i.e. give up my life)

gold to pay my legions: (every army was privately-owned)

covetous: grasping

rascal counters: worthless pieces

rived: split/broken

infirmities: weaknesses

BRUTUS   If you did, I care not.

CASSIUS   When Cæsar lived, he durst not thus have
                  moved me.

BRUTUS   Peace, peace, you durst not so have tempted him.

CASSIUS   I durst not?   60

BRUTUS   No.

CASSIUS   What, durst not tempt him?

BRUTUS   For your life you durst not.

CASSIUS   Do not presume too much upon my love;
           I may do that I shall be sorry for.

BRUTUS   You have done that you should be sorry for.
           There is no terror, Cassius, in your threats;
           For I am armed so strong in honesty
           That they pass by me as the idle wind,
           Which I respect not. I did send to you
           For certain sums of gold, which you denied me;   70
           For I can raise no money by vile means.
           By heaven, I had rather coin my heart,
           And drop my blood for drachmas, than to wring
           From the hard hands of peasants their vile trash
           By any indirection. I did send
           To you for gold to pay my legions,
           Which you denied me. Was that done like
                  Cassius?
           Should I have answered Caius Cassius so?
           When Marcus Brutus grows so covetous,
           To lock such rascal counters from his friends,   80
           Be ready gods with all your thunderbolts:
           Dash him to pieces.

CASSIUS   I denied you not.

BRUTUS   You did.

CASSIUS   I did not. He was but a fool that brought
           My answer back. Brutus hath rived my heart.
           A friend should bear his friend's infirmities;
           But Brutus makes mine greater than they are.

Cassius is moved by Brutus' criticism, and asks Brutus to kill him. They are reconciled.

Olympus: see p112
braved: defied
checked: rebuked
conned by rote: learned by heart
Pluto: king (therefore wealthy) of the underworld
be'st: are
scope: range, room to move
dishonour shall be humour: any disgrace will be put down to your state of mind
yoked: joined
enforced: pressed

BRUTUS	I do not, till you practise them on me.
CASSIUS	You love me not.
BRUTUS	I do not like your faults.
CASSIUS	A friendly eye could never see such faults.

90

BRUTUS	A flatterer's would not, though they do appear As huge as high Olympus.
CASSIUS	Come Antony, and young Octavius come, Revenge yourselves alone on Cassius, For Cassius is aweary of the world: Hated by one he loves; braved by his brother; Checked like a bondman; all his faults observed, Set in a note-book, learned, and conned by rote. To cast into my teeth. O I could weep My spirit from mine eyes. There is my dagger, And here my naked breast; within, a heart Dearer than Pluto's mine, richer than gold. If that thou be'st a Roman, take it forth. I that denied thee gold, will give my heart. Strike as thou didst at Cæsar. For I know, When thou didst hate him worst, thou lovedst him better Than ever thou lovedst Cassius.

100

BRUTUS	Sheathe your dagger. Be angry when you will, it shall have scope. Do what you will, dishonour shall be humour. O Cassius, you are yoked with a lamb That carries anger as the flint bears fire, Who much enforced shows a hasty spark, And straight is cold again.

110

CASSIUS	Hath Cassius lived To be but mirth and laughter to his Brutus, When grief and blood ill-tempered vexeth him?
BRUTUS	When I spoke that, I was ill-tempered too.
CASSIUS	Do you confess so much? Give me your hand.
BRUTUS	And my heart too.

**Brutus says he will make allowances in future for
Cassius' quick temper. A poet comes as peacemaker
and he is thrown out.**

rash humour: quick temper
chides: rebukes, tells off
cynic: philosopher who denounces pleasure
fashion: way of speaking
companion: fellow

CASSIUS	O Brutus
BRUTUS	What's the matter?
CASSIUS	Have not you love enough to bear with me,
	When that rash humour which my mother gave
	me
	Makes me forgetful?

120

BRUTUS	Yes Cassius, and from henceforth,
	When you are over-earnest with your Brutus,
	He'll think your mother chides, and leave you so.

Enter POET, *followed by* LUCILIUS, TITINIUS, *and* LUCIUS

POET	Let me go in to see the generals.
	There is some grudge between 'em, 'tis not meet
	They be alone.
LUCILIUS	You shall not come to them.
POET	Nothing but death shall stay me.
CASSIUS	How now? What's the matter?
POET	For shame you generals, what do you mean?

130

	Love, and be friends, as two such men should be,
	For I have seen more years I'm sure than ye.
CASSIUS	Ha, ha, how vilely doth this cynic rhyme!
BRUTUS	Get you hence sirrah. Saucy fellow, hence!
CASSIUS	Bear with him Brutus, 'tis his fashion.
BRUTUS	I'll know his humour, when he knows his time.
	What should the wars do with these jigging fools?
	Companion, hence!
CASSIUS	Away, away, be gone.

[*Exit Poet*

BRUTUS	Lucilius and Titinius, bid the commanders
	Prepare to lodge their companies tonight.

140

CASSIUS	And come yourselves, and bring Messala with
	you
	Immediately to us.

Brutus tells Cassius that Portia is dead.

give place to accidental evils: take notice of distractions, insignificant events
How 'scaped I killing?: why did you not kill me?
insupportable: inconsolable
touching: (it touches Cassius too)
tidings: news
distract: mad
swallowed fire: Plutarch, the historian, reports she choked on burning coals

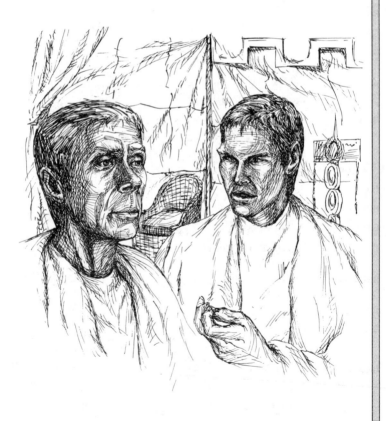

[Exeunt LUCILIUS *and* TITINIUS

BRUTUS   Lucius, a bowl of wine.

[Exit LUCIUS

CASSIUS   I did not think you could have been so angry.

BRUTUS   O Cassius, I am sick of many griefs.

CASSIUS   Of your philosophy you make no use,
If you give place to accidental evils.

BRUTUS   No man bears sorrow better. Portia is dead.

CASSIUS   Ha! Portia?

BRUTUS   She is dead.

CASSIUS   How 'scaped I killing when I crossed you so?   150
O insupportable and touching loss!
Upon what sickness?

BRUTUS   Impatient of my absence,
And grief that young Octavius with Mark Antony
Have made themselves so strong; for with her
      death
That tidings came. With this she fell distract,
And, her attendants absent, swallowed fire.

CASSIUS   And died so?

BRUTUS   Even so.

CASSIUS   O ye immortal gods!

Enter LUCIUS *with wine and tapers*

BRUTUS   Speak no more of her. Give me a bowl of wine.
In this I bury all unkindness Cassius.

CASSIUS   My heart is thirsty for that noble pledge.   160
Fill Lucius, till the wine o'erswell the cup.
I cannot drink too much of Brutus' love.

BRUTUS   Come in Titinius.

[Exit Lucius

Enter LUCILIUS, TITINIUS, *with* MESSALA

Brutus, Cassius, Titinius and Messala meet to discuss tactics. Messala reports on the purge in Rome. He has news confirming the death of Portia.

taper: candle
call ... necessities: sort out our priorities
Bending: aiming
Philippi: (Phigh-lip-pie)
tenor: meaning
proscription: death penalty
bills of outlawry: papers sentencing people to be outlawed
aught: anything
meditating ... once: having considered that she had to die
    sometime

	Welcome good Messala.
	Now sit we close about this taper here,
	And call in question our necessities.
CASSIUS	Portia, art thou gone?
BRUTUS	No more I pray you.
	Messala, I have here received letters,
	That young Octavius and Mark Antony
	Come down upon us with a mighty power,
	Bending their expedition toward Philippi.
MESSALA	Myself have letters of the selfsame tenor.
BRUTUS	With what addition?
MESSALA	That by proscription and bills of outlawry,
	Octavius, Antony, and Lepidus,
	Have put to death an hundred senators.
BRUTUS	Therein our letters do not well agree.
	Mine speak of seventy senators that died
	By their proscriptions, Cicero being one.
CASSIUS	Cicero one?
MESSALA	Cicero is dead,
	And by that order of proscription.
	Had you your letters from your wife, my lord?
BRUTUS	No Messala.
MESSALA	Nor nothing in your letters writ of her?
BRUTUS	Nothing Messala.
MESSALA	That methinks is strange.
BRUTUS	Why ask you? Hear you aught of her in yours?
MESSALA	No my lord.
BRUTUS	Now as you are a Roman tell me true.
MESSALA	Then like a Roman bear the truth I tell,
	For certain she is dead, and by strange manner.
BRUTUS	Why farewell Portia. We must die, Messala.
	With meditating that she must die once,
	I have the patience to endure it now.
MESSALA	Even so great men great losses should endure.

Line numbers in right margin: 170, 180, 190

Brutus and Cassius disagree about a strategy for battle but decide on Brutus' plan.

art: philosophy, a way of looking at life

to our work alive: back to the business of living (in contrast to Portia, who is dead)

marching to Philippi: in reality this journey took about eight months

means: resources (money, food)

offence: harm

Do stand ... affection: are not really on our side

we have tried ... friends: we have sought help from every friend we have

contribution: help

There is a tide ... ventures: a metaphor from sea travel. On coasts which were shallow, ships had to wait for a high tide before they could leave harbour. He means: if we act when the time suits us we can be successful. If we miss the opportunity we lose everything.

CASSIUS   I have as much of this in art as you,
              But yet my nature could not bear it so.

BRUTUS   Well, to our work alive. What do you think
              Of marching to Philippi presently?

CASSIUS   I do not think it good.

BRUTUS   Your reason?

CASSIUS   This it is:
              'Tis better that the enemy seek us;
              So shall he waste his means, weary his soldiers,   200
              Doing himself offence, whilst we lying still,
              Are full of rest, defence, and nimbleness.

BRUTUS   Good reasons must of force give place to better.
              The people 'twixt Philippi and this ground
              Do stand but in a forced affection;
              For they have grudged us contribution.
              The enemy, marching along by them,
              By them shall make a fuller number up,
              Come on refreshed, new-added, and encouraged;
              From which advantage shall we cut him off,   210
              If at Philippi we do face him there,
              These people at our back.

CASSIUS   Hear me good brother.

BRUTUS   Under your pardon. You must note beside,
              That we have tried the utmost of our friends,
              Our legions are brim-full, our cause is ripe.
              The enemy increaseth every day;
              We, at the height, are ready to decline.
              There is a tide in the affairs of men,
              Which taken at the flood leads on to fortune;
              Omitted, all the voyage of their life   220
              Is bound in shallows and in miseries.
              On such a full sea are we now afloat,
              And we must take the current when it serves,
              Or lose our ventures.

CASSIUS   Then with your will go on.
              We'll along ourselves, and meet them at Philippi.

Brutus calls for two soldiers to sleep in his tent in case he needs to send a message to Cassius.

---

niggard: be niggardly/sparing (i.e. nature says we should
    sleep but we shall only take a little rest)
never (again) **come**
o'erwatched: awake too long

BRUTUS The deep of night is crept upon our talk,
And nature must obey necessity,
Which we will niggard with a little rest.
There is no more to say.

CASIUS No more. Good night:
Early tomorrow will we rise, and hence.   230

BRUTUS Lucius! [*Enter* LUCIUS] My gown. [*Exit Lucius*]
Farewell good Messala:
Good night Titinius. Noble, noble Cassius,
Good night, and good repose.

CASSIUS O my dear brother!
This was an ill beginning of the night.
Never come such division 'tween our souls!
Let it not Brutus.

[*Enter* LUCIUS *with gown*

BRUTUS Every thing is well.

CASSIUS Good night my lord.

BRUTUS Good night good brother.

TITINIUS, MESSALA Good night Lord Brutus.

BRUTUS Farewell every one.

[*Exeunt Cassius, Titinius, Lucilius and Messala*

Give me the gown. Where is thy instrument?

LUCIUS Here in the tent.

BRUTUS What, thou speak'st drowsily?   240
Poor knave, I blame thee not; thou art o'er watched.
Call Claudius and some other of my men;
I'll have them sleep on cushions in my tent.

LUCIUS Varro and Claudius!

Enter VARRO *and* CLAUDIUS

VARRO Calls my lord?

BRUTUS I pray you sirs, lie in my tent and sleep;
It may be I shall raise you by and by

Brutus reads. Cæsar's ghost appears.

watch: await
bethink: change my mind
an't: if it
might: strength
young bloods: young men
leaden mace: heavy club
leaf: page

	On business to my brother Cassius.
VARRO	So please you, we will stand and watch your pleasure.
BRUTUS	I will not have it so. Lie down good sirs; 250 It may be I shall otherwise bethink me. Look Lucius, here's the book I sought for so; I put it in the pocket of my gown.
LUCIUS	I was sure your lordship did not give it me.
BRUTUS	Bear with me good boy, I am much forgetful. Canst thou hold up thy heavy eyes awhile, And touch thy instrument a strain or two?
LUCIUS	Ay my lord, an't please you.
BRUTUS	It does, my boy. I trouble thee too much, but thou art willing.
LUCIUS	It is my duty sir. 260
BRUTUS	I should not urge thy duty past thy might; I know young bloods look for a time of rest.
LUCIUS	I have slept my lord already.
BRUTUS	It was well done, and thou shalt sleep again; I will not hold thee long. If I do live, I will be good to thee.

[Music and a song

This is a sleepy tune. O murd'rous slumber,
Layest thou thy leaden mace upon my boy,
That plays thee music? Gentle knave good night;
I will not do thee so much wrong to wake thee.   270
If thou dost nod, thou break'st thy instrument;
I'll take it from thee; and, good boy, good night.
Let me see, let me see; is not the leaf turned down
Where I left reading? Here it is, I think.

Enter the Ghost of CÆSAR

How ill this taper burns. Ha! Who comes here?
I think it is the weakness of mine eyes

The ghost promises to be at Philippi. Brutus wakes the others to ask if they have seen anything.

apparition: ghost
to stare: stand on end
evil spirit: spirit reminding Brutus of his evil, or Cæsar's spirit promising to dominate Brutus' spirit; or both.
false: out of tune
sirrah: term of address – 'You, man, …'

	That shapes this monstrous apparition.
	It comes upon me. Art thou any thing?
	Art thou some god, some angel, or some devil,
	That mak'st my blood cold, and my hair to stare? 280
	Speak to me what thou art.
GHOST	Thy evil spirit Brutus.
BRUTUS	Why com'st thou?
GHOST	To tell thee thou shalt see me at Philippi.
BRUTUS	Well; then I shall see thee again?
GHOST	Ay, at Philippi.
BRUTUS	Why I will see thee at Philippi then.

[*Exit Ghost*

	Now I have taken heart thou vanishest.
	Ill spirit, I would hold more talk with thee.
	Boy, Lucius! Varro! Claudius! Sirs, awake. 290
	Claudius!
LUCIUS	The strings, my lord, are false.
BRUTUS	He thinks he still is at his instrument. Lucius, awake.
LUCIUS	My lord.
BRUTUS	Didst thou dream, Lucius, that thou so criedst out?
LUCIUS	My lord, I do not know that I did cry.
BRUTUS	Yes that thou didst. Didst thou see any thing?
LUCIUS	Nothing my lord. 300
BRUTUS	Sleep again Lucius. Sirrah Claudius! [*To* VARRO] Fellow thou, awake!
VARRO	My lord.
CLAUDIUS	My lord.
BRUTUS	Why did you so cry out sirs, in your sleep?
VARRO, CLAUDIUS	Did we my lord?
BRUTUS	Ay. Saw you any thing?
VARRO	No my lord, I saw nothing.

Brutus sends a message for Cassius to get his men on the march.

commend me: give my greetings
betimes: early
before: ahead

ACTIVITIES

Keeping track

Scene 1

1 Why and how do Antony and Octavius disagree about Lepidus?

Scene 2

2 What are the early signs that things are not well between Brutus and Cassius?

Scene 3

3 What is Cassius' particular complaint?
4 In lines 56–57 Cassius accuses Brutus of misquoting him. What did Cassius actually say? What did he mean? Who, then, is right at this point?
5 What is Brutus' complaint against Cassius?
6 How does Cassius show remorse?
7 Messala is impressed (line 193) by the way Brutus reacts to his 'news' (line 190) . Thinking about it later, however, Messala might suspect Brutus knew already. Why?

CLAUDIUS   Nor I my lord.

BRUTUS   Go and commend me to my brother Cassius.
        Bid him set on his powers betimes before,   310
        And we will follow.

BOTH   It shall be done my lord.

                            [*Exeunt*

8 The ghost of Cæsar would probably have more effect on
the Elizabethan audience than it appears to have on Brutus
at first. Can you suggest why he seems to take it so calmly?

Discussion

1 What are the triumvirate doing at the beginning of Act 4
scene 1? Why do you think they are doing that? Can you
suggest how they might decide on whom to include?

2 Brutus' plan for battle is agreed to, but Cassius' has its
merits, too (Act 4 scene 3). Which idea would you have
chosen? Why?

Drama

'Their names are pricked'

Groups of five.

Lepidus consents to the naming of his brother as a traitor and
agrees he should die. His brother probably feels reasonably
safe.

1 You are five soldiers who have been told to go to Lepidus' brother's house and kill him. (Decide if you have to kill his family as well.) Discuss how you propose to carry out this unpleasant task. Who will lead you? Are you expecting much resistance? Are you going to try to trick him into leaving his house so that he can be killed with less trouble?

2 Now imagine you are Lepidus' family sitting down to dinner, when a servant arrives, breathless, with a warning that soldiers are coming. What will you do? 'Die like Romans' or run away? Will you be able to escape? Discuss the situation.

3 When you have established the two situations, keep changing from one to the other, getting nearer and nearer to the moment of confrontation. Do about five visits to each group of people making each visit shorter until the last two are only for a few seconds. This will help you to build up the tension.

4 Continue this until the moment of the first blow, then stop and make a still image of this moment (see p237).

5 Then imagine what the scene would look like after the killing is over. Make a still image of that.

6 Share your work with the rest of the class.

7 Discuss what this tells you about Octavius, Mark Antony and Lepidus.

Character

1 What do Antony's comments about Lepidus tell us about Antony himself?

2 The disagreement between Brutus and Cassius emphasises their differences as men. Who is to blame for the quarrel? Who is in control? Who is on the defensive? Is this because of the strength of the arguments, or the character of the person involved? Look especially at Act 4 scene 3, lines 42–50, 63–70 and 93–107.

3 Bring up to date your Character logs on Brutus, Cassius and Antony. Close your log on Cæsar.

Close study

1 When Cassius and Brutus part, one says 'my lord' and the other says 'good brother'.
   - Does this tell us more about the relationship between the two of them?
   - How do they think about each other?
   - Do they see themselves as equals, or not?
   - Are there any reasons why one should feel superior, or inferior, to the other?
2 In Act 4 we see Brutus being faced with a succession of problems which depress him to some extent. Look at the list and decide which was probably most depressing, which next, and so on down to the least depressing. Explain why you chose a particular problem as the most depressing.
   - Cassius' past behaviour
   - Cassius' present attitude
   - Portia's death
   - Cassius' accusations
   - the poet's interruption
   - news of the death of 100 senators
   - news of the approaching armies
   - Cæsar's ghost.

Writing

Enter the Ghost of Cæsar

We know that the audiences of Shakespeare's time were superstitious and they would probably accept the ghost as readily as they accepted other characters. Today, however, more sophisticated theatre audiences demand convincing ghosts. And the entrance of the ghost is vital if the audience is to take it seriously.

If you were director:
- what would your ghost look like? (make-up, costume, appearance)
- how would your ghost enter? (trap-door? already hidden on stage? in a cloud of 'dry ice'?)
- would you need special lighting, music, perhaps?

Make brief notes about how you see the ghost being presented best.

Cæsar Deserved To Die!

You are one of the conspirators in hiding. It is only a matter of time before you are caught. You decide to write an explanation of your actions for your family to read. In the first section mention those qualities of Cæsar which the general public admired. In the second section write about the Cæsar you knew, and those things about him which caused you to join the conspiracy because you felt he deserved to die. (Your Character log will help you with this writing)

Quiz

Who said the following, and to whom?
1 'Most noble brother, you have done me wrong'
2   'you yourself
   Are much condemned to have an itching palm'
3 'Why, I will see thee at Philippi then'

Who said the following about whom?
4 'This is a slight unmeritable man
   Meet to be sent on errands'
5 'Speak no more of her. Give me a bowl of wine'
6 ''Tis better that the enemy seek us
   So shall he waste his means, weary his soldiers'

Say all you can about the following (who said it; what it means; what it refers to).

7 'So is my horse, Octavius and for that
   I do appoint him store of provender.
   It is a creature that I teach to fight,
   To wind, to stop, to run directly on.'

8   'we are at the stake
   And bayed about with many enemies
   And some that smile have in their hearts, I fear
   Millions of mischiefs.'

9   'What shall one of us
   That struck the foremost man of all this world,
   But for supporting robbers, shall we now
   Contaminate our fingers with base bribes?'

10   'He was but a fool that brought
   My answer back. Brutus hath rived my heart.
   A friend should bear his friend's infirmities,
   But Brutus makes mine greater than they are.'

Octavius and Antony learn that Brutus and Cassius are approaching. They decide on a battle plan.

battles: battalions
warn: summon
Answering ... them: taking the offensive, attacking first
I am in their bosoms: I know their thoughts
fearful bravery: formidable forces
fasten in our thoughts: make us think
bloody sign of battle: war flag
even: equally balanced
upon the right hand: the stronger/strongest general always
    fought at the right hand end of the battle line
cross: contradict/cross over (play on words)
exigent: emergency, crisis

Act five

The plains of Philippi
Enter OCTAVIUS, ANTONY, *and their* Army

OCTAVIUS   Now Antony, our hopes are answered.
You said the enemy would not come down,
But keep the hills and upper regions.
It proves not so; their battles are at hand;
They mean to warn us at Philippi here,
Answering before we do demand of them.

ANTONY   Tut, I am in their bosoms, and I know
Wherefore they do it. They could be content
To visit other places, and come down   10
With fearful bravery, thinking by this face
To fasten in our thoughts that they have courage;
But 'tis not so.

[*Enter a* MESSENGER

MESSENGER   Prepare you generals.
The enemy comes on in gallant show;
Their bloody sign of battle is hung out,
And something to be done immediately.

ANTONY   Octavius, lead your battle softly on,
Upon the left hand of the even field.

OCTAVIUS   Upon the right hand I, keep thou the left.

ANTONY   Why do you cross me in this exigent?

OCTAVIUS   I do not cross you; but I will do so.   20

[*March*

The four generals meet to talk before the battle, but merely exchange insults.

stand: halt
parley: talk
answer on their charge: do as they want
bad strokes (Brutus): unnecessary conflict
bad strokes (Antony): evil blows
posture of your blows: your method of attack
Hybla: a mountain in Sicily, famous for honey
very wisely ... sting: you are all talk
fawned: grovelled
cur: dog
thank yourself: you are to blame

Drum. Enter BRUTUS, CASSIUS, *and their* Army;
LUCILIUS, TITINIUS, MESSALA, *and others*

BRUTUS   They stand, and would have parley.

CASSIUS   Stand fast Titinius, we must out and talk.

OCTAVIUS   Mark Antony, shall we give sign of battle?

ANTONY   No Cæsar, we will answer on their charge.
              Make forth; the generals would have some
                  words.

OCTAVIUS   Stir not until the signal.

BRUTUS   Words before blows; is it so, countrymen?

OCTAVIUS   Not that we love words better, as you do.

BRUTUS   Good words are better than bad strokes,
                  Octavius.

ANTONY   In your bad strokes, Brutus, you give good   30
                  words:
              Witness the hole you made in Cæsar's heart,
              Crying 'Long live! hail Cæsar!'

CASSIUS   Antony,
              The posture of your blows are yet unknown;
              But for your words, they rob the Hybla bees,
              And leave them honeyless.

ANTONY   Not stingless too.

BRUTUS   O yes, and soundless too;
              For you have stol'n their buzzing, Antony,
              And very wisely threat before you sting.

ANTONY   Villains, you did not so, when your vile daggers
              Hacked one another in the sides of Cæsar.   40
              You showed your teeth like apes, and fawned
                  like hounds,
              And bowed like bondmen, kissing Cæsar's feet;
              Whilst damned Casca, like a cur, behind
              Struck Cæsar on the neck. O you flatterers!

CASSIUS   Flatterers? Now Brutus thank yourself;
              This tongue had not offended so today,

After further insults, Octavius and Antony leave to prepare for battle.

might have ruled: had been listened to
the cause: get to the point
proof: outcome
another Cæsar...traitors: you have killed me
so I hope: i.e. that he cannot die by 'traitors' hands'
peevish: irritable
masker: someone who took part in masques, dances and
    other entertainments in which the dancers wore masks.
reveller: (Antony had a reputation as a playboy)
Old Cassius still: still showing spite
stomachs: an appetite for fighting
bark: a boat
on the hazard: at stake

	If Cassius might have ruled.
OCTAVIUS	Come, come, the cause. If arguing make us sweat,
	The proof of it will turn to redder drops.
	Look, 50
	I draw a sword against conspirators;
	When think you that the sword goes up again?
	Never, till Cæsar's three and thirty wounds
	Be well avenged; or till another Cæsar
	Have added slaughter to the sword of traitors.
BRUTUS	Cæsar, thou canst not die by traitors' hands,
	Unless thou bring'st them with thee.
OCTAVIUS	So I hope.
	I was not born to die on Brutus' sword.
BRUTUS	O if thou wert the noblest of thy strain,
	Young man, thou couldst not die more honourable. 60
CASSIUS	A peevish schoolboy, worthless of such honour,
	Joined with a masker and a reveller.
ANTONY	Old Cassius still.
OCTAVIUS	Come Antony, away!
	Defiance, traitors, hurl we in your teeth.
	If you dare fight today, come to the field;
	If not, when you have stomachs.

[*Exeunt Octavius, Antony, and their army*

CASSIUS	Why now, blow wind, swell billow, and swim bark.
	The storm is up, and all is on the hazard.
BRUTUS	Ho Lucilius, hark, a word with you.
LUCILIUS	My lord.

[*Brutus and Lucilius talk apart*

CASSIUS	Messala.
MESSALA	What says my general? 70

**Cassius tells Messala he has become superstitious. He
is in good heart but persuades Brutus to think about
defeat.**

compelled: forced

set upon...liberties: the liberty of our country will be
decided in one battle

Epicurus: a Greek philosopher who believed that life was
to be enjoyed. The Epicureans and the Stoics scorned the
supernatural.

credit...presage: believe in omens

ensign: standard, flag

consorted: escorted, came with

steads: places

sickly: about to die

canopy: covering

fatal: deadly

but: only

fresh of spirit: in good heart

constantly: firmly

lead on our days to age: grow old

still: always

let's reason ... befall: let's decide what to do if the worst
happens

philosophy: as a Stoic, Brutus considers suicide cowardly

Cato: Portia's father (p85) committed suicide and others
have followed his example

vile: morally wrong

CASSIUS   Messala,
This is my birthday; at this very day
Was Cassius born. Give me thy hand Messala.
Be thou my witness that against my will,
As Pompey was, am I compelled to set
Upon one battle all our liberties.
You know that I held Epicurus strong,
And his opinion; now I change my mind,
And partly credit things that do presage.
Coming from Sardis, on our former ensign   80
Two mighty eagles fell, and there they perched,
Gorging and feeding from our soldiers' hands,
Who to Philippi here consorted us.
This morning are they fled away and gone,
And in their steads do ravens, crows, and kites,
Fly o'er our heads, and downward look on us
As we were sickly prey: their shadows seem
A canopy most fatal, under which
Our army lies, ready to give up the ghost.

MESSALA   Believe not so.

CASSIUS   I but believe it partly,   90
For I am fresh of spirit and resolved
To meet all perils very constantly.

BRUTUS   Even so Lucilius.

CASSIUS   Now most noble Brutus,
The gods today stand friendly, that we may,
Lovers in peace, lead on our days to age.
But since the affairs of men rest still incertain,
Let's reason with the worst that may befall.
If we do lose this battle, then is this
The very last time we shall speak together.
What are you then determined to do?   100

BRUTUS   Even by the rule of that philosophy
By which I did blame Cato for the death
Which he did give himself. I know not how,
But I do find it cowardly and vile,

Brutus disapproves of suicide but he is determined not to be a captive. Brutus and Cassius part to do battle.

prevent the time of life: cut short one's life-span
stay the providence: await the fate decreed
ere: before
sufficeth: is enough

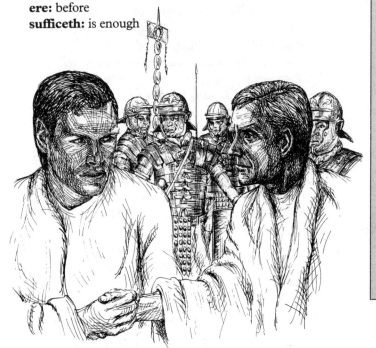

Brutus orders his troops to attack when he sees Octavius weak.

bills: orders
other side: Cassius' wing

For fear of what might fall, so to prevent
The time of life - arming myself with patience
To stay the providence of some high powers
That govern us below.

CASSIUS   Then, if we lose this battle,
You are contented to be led in triumph
Through the streets of Rome?   110

BRUTUS   No Cassius, no. Think not, thou noble Roman,
That ever Brutus will go bound to Rome;
He bears too great a mind. But this same day
Must end that work the ides of March begun;
And whether we shall meet again I know not.
Therefore our everlasting farewell take.
For ever, and for ever, farewell Cassius.
If we do meet again, why we shall smile;
If not, why then this parting was well made.

CASSIUS   For ever, and for ever, farewell Brutus.   120
If we do meet again, we'll smile indeed;
If not, 'tis true this parting was well made.

BRUTUS   Why then lead on. O that a man might know
The end of this day's business ere it come.
But it sufficeth that the day will end,
And then the end is known. Come ho, away!

                                     [*Exeunt*

SCENE 2

The battlefield
Alarum. Enter BRUTUS *and* MESSALA

BRUTUS   Ride, ride, Messala, ride and give these bills
Unto the legions on the other side.

[*Loud alarm*

Let them set on at once; for I perceive

cold demeanour: low spirits

Cassius' troops are fleeing. Pindarus urges Cassius to flee, too, because Antony is in Cassius' camp.

villains: his own men
ensign: standard-bearer
spoil: plunder
even with a thought: as quickly as thinking

But cold demeanour in Octavius' wing,
And sudden push gives them the overthrow.
Ride, ride, Messala, let them all come down.

[*Exeunt*

SCENE **3**

The battlefield
Alarums. Enter CASSIUS *and* TITINIUS

CASSIUS
O look, Titinius, look, the villains fly.
Myself have to mine own turned enemy:
This ensign here of mine was turning back;
I slew the coward, and did take it from him.

TITINIUS
O Cassius, Brutus gave the word too early,
Who having some advantage on Octavius,
Took it too eagerly; his soldiers fell to spoil,
Whilst we by Antony are all enclosed.

Enter PINDARUS

PINDARUS
Fly further off my lord, fly further off;
Mark Antony is in your tents my lord: 10
Fly therefore noble Cassius, fly far off.

CASSIUS
This hill is far enough. Look, look Titinius;
Are those my tents where I perceive the fire?

TITINIUS
They are, my lord.

CASSIUS
                                    Titinius, if thou lovest me,
Mount thou my horse, and hide thy spurs in
     him,
Till he have brought thee up to yonder troops
And here again, that I may rest assured
Whether yond troops are friend or enemy.   20

TITINIUS
I will be here again, even with a thought.

[*Exit*

Pindarus observes events from a hill-top. He informs Cassius that Titinius has been taken. Cassius orders Pindarus to kill him.

thick: blurred
notest: notice
run his compass: come full circle
light: dismount
Parthia: (today the Middle East) where Cassius had conducted a successful campaign, more than ten years previously
freeman: by keeping his promise, Pindarus will free himself of all obligations to Cassius

CASSIUS	Go Pindarus, get higher on that hill. 20
	My sight was ever thick. Regard Titinius,
	And tell me what thou notest about the field.

[*Exit Pindarus*

This day I breathed first: time is come round,
And where I did begin, there shall I end;
My life is run his compass. Sirrah, what news?

PINDARUS	[*Above*] O my lord!
CASSIUS	What news?
PINDARUS	[*Above*] Titinius is enclosed round about
	With horsemen, that make to him on the spur,
	Yet he spurs on. Now they are almost on him. 30
	Now Titinius! Now some light. O he lights too.
	He's ta'en. [*Shout*] And hark! they shout for joy.
CASSIUS	Come down, behold no more.
	O coward that I am, to live so long.
	To see my best friend ta'en before my face.

[PINDARUS *descends*

Come hither sirrah.
In Parthia did I take thee prisoner,
And then I swore thee, saving of thy life,
That whatsoever I did bid thee do,
Thou shouldst attempt it. Come now, keep thine
     oath. 40
Now be a freeman, and with this good sword
That ran through Cæsar's bowels, search this
     bosom.
Stand not to answer. Here, take thou the hilts,
And when my face is covered, as 'tis now,
Guide thou the sword - Cæsar, thou art
     revenged,
Even with the sword that killed thee.

[*Dies*

Pindarus flees. Titinius and Messala, returning with good news, discover the body.

durst: dared

change: exchange

These tidings: this news

disconsolate: sorrowful

O my heart!: (Cassius referred to Titinius as his best friend)

Our day is gone: the light has gone out

our deeds are done: we are no longer effective

good: (the only change from the previous sentence, for emphasis)

apt: easily deceived

O hateful Error...engendered thee: sadness makes people jump to the wrong conclusions, with tragic results. (Cassius' mood, melancholy, gave birth to error. It is this error that has killed Cassius).

PINDARUS   So, I am free; yet would not so have been,
Durst I have done my will. O Cassius!
Far from this country Pindarus shall run,
Where never Roman shall take note of him.   50

                                        [Exit

Enter TITINIUS *and* MESSALA

MESSALA   It is but change, Titinius; for Octavius
Is overthrown by noble Brutus' power,
As Cassius' legions are by Antony.

TITINIUS   These tidings will well comfort Cassius.

MESSALA   Where did you leave him?

TITINIUS   All disconsolate,
With Pindarus his bondman, on this hill.

MESSALA   Is not that he that lies upon the ground?

TITINIUS   He lies not like the living. O my heart!

MESSALA   Is not that he?

TITINIUS   No, this was he, Messala,
But Cassius is no more. O setting sun,   60
As in thy red rays thou dost sink tonight,
So in his red blood Cassius' day is set.
The sun of Rome is set. Our day is gone;
Clouds, dews, and dangers come; our deeds are
   done:
Mistrust of my success hath done this deed.

MESSALA   Mistrust of good success hath done this deed.
O hateful Error, Melancholy's child,
Why dost thou show to the apt thoughts of men
The things that are not? O Error soon conceived,
Thou never com'st unto a happy birth,   70
But kill'st the mother that engendered thee.

TITINIUS   What Pindarus! Where art thou Pindarus?

MESSALA   Seek him Titinius, whilst I go to meet
The noble Brutus, thrusting this report
Into his ears; I may say thrusting it;

Messala goes to inform Brutus. Titinius kills himself alongside Cassius. Brutus sees the influence of Cæsar's ghost in these deaths.

envenomed: poisoned
hie: hurry
misconstrued: misunderstood
garland: victory wreath
apace: quickly
part: what is expected of him
own proper entrails: very own innards
where: whether, if

For piercing steel, and darts envenomed
Shall be as welcome to the ears of Brutus
As tidings of this sight.

TITINIUS   Hie you Messala,
And I will seek for Pindarus the while.

[*Exit Messala*

Why didst thou send me forth, brave Cassius?   80
Did I not meet thy friends, and did not they
Put on my brows this wreath of victory,
And bid me give it thee? Didst thou not hear
    their shouts?
Alas, thou hast misconstrued every thing.
But hold thee, take this garland on thy brow;
Thy Brutus bid me give it thee, and I
Will do his bidding. Brutus, come apace,
And see how I regarded Caius Cassius.
By your leave, gods - this is a Roman's part.
Come Cassius' sword, and find Titinius' heart.   90

[*Dies*

Alarum. Enter MESSALA, *with* BRUTUS, YOUNG
CATO, STRATO, VOLUMNIUS, LUCILIUS, LABEO, *and*
FLAVIUS

BRUTUS   Where, where Messala, doth his body lie?

MESSALA   Lo yonder, and Titinius mourning it.

BRUTUS   Titinius' face is upward.

CATO   He is slain.

BRUTUS   O Julius Cæsar, thou art mighty yet;
Thy spirit walks abroad, and turns our swords
In our own proper entrails.

[*Low alarums*

CATO   Brave Titinius!
Look where he have not crowned dead Cassius.

Brutus speaks over the bodies. He declares his intention to fight again before the day is out.

Thasos: island near Philippi
funerals: funeral ceremonies
discomfort us: lowers our spirits
battles: troops
ere: before
try fortune: test fate
second fight: (historically, the second battle of Philippi took place twenty days later)

Brutus rallies his men. Lucilius pretends to be Brutus.

bastard: no true Roman
my country's friend: i.e. not a traitor

BRUTUS   Are yet two Romans living such as these?

The last of all the Romans, fare thee well.

It is impossible that ever Rome   100

Should breed thy fellow. Friends, I owe more
     tears

To this dead man than you shall see me pay.

I shall find time, Cassius, I shall find time.

Come therefore, and to Thasos send his body.

His funerals shall not be in our camp,

Lest it discomfort us. Lucilius come,

And come young Cato, let us to the field.

Labeo and Flavius, set our battles on.

'Tis three o'clock; and Romans, yet ere night

We shall try fortune in a second fight.   110

                       [*Exeunt*

SCENE **4**

The battlefield
Alarum. Enter BRUTUS, MESSALA, YOUNG CATO,
LUCILIUS, *and* FLAVIUS

BRUTUS   Yet countrymen, O yet hold up your heads.

                       [*Exit*

CATO   What bastard doth not? Who will go with me?

I will proclaim my name about the field.

I am the son of Marcus Cato, ho!

A foe to tyrants, and my country's friend.

I am the son of Marcus Cato, ho!

Enter Soldiers and fight

LUCILIUS   And I am Brutus, Marcus Brutus, I;

Brutus my country's friend; know me for Brutus!

Cato is killed. Lucilius is captured. Antony admires Lucilius' spirit.

I yield to die: I give in to death
There is so much ... death: There is a lot to be gained from killing me right away; killing Brutus will bring great honour.
Room ho!: make room
like: true to
where: whether
is chanced: has turned out

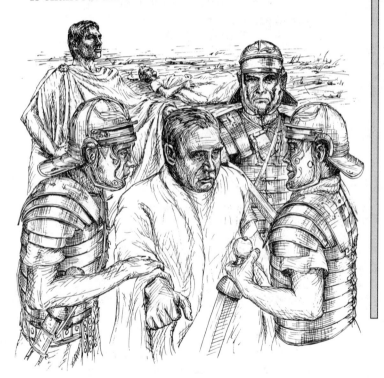

O young and noble Cato, art thou down?
Why now thou diest as bravely as Titinius,   10
And mayst be honoured, being Cato's son.

1ST SOLDIER Yield, or thou diest.

LUCILIUS   Only I yield to die.
There is so much that thou wilt kill me straight;
Kill Brutus, and be honoured in his death.

1ST SOLDIER We must not. A noble prisoner.

2ND SOLDIER Room ho! Tell Antony, Brutus is ta'en.

1ST SOLDIER I'll tell the news. Here comes the general.

Enter ANTONY

Brutus is ta'en, Brutus is ta'en my lord.

ANTONY Where is he?

LUCILIUS Safe Antony, Brutus is safe enough.   20
I dare assure thee that no enemy
Shall ever take alive the noble Brutus
The gods defend him from so great a shame.
When you do find him, or alive or dead,
He will be found like Brutus, like himself.

ANTONY This is not Brutus, friend, but I assure you,
A prize no less in worth; keep this man safe,
Give him all kindness. I had rather have
Such men my friends than enemies. Go on,
And see where Brutus be alive or dead;   30
And bring us word unto Octavius' tent
How every thing is chanced.

                                        [*Exeunt*

**It is night. Brutus is cornered, away from his camp.
He asks his followers, in turn, to kill him. Cæsar's
ghost has appeared to him again.**

remains: survivors
poor remains of friends: (it seems Brutus has accepted
 defeat)
Statilius: Statilius crept through the enemy lines to find out
 what the situation was at Brutus' camp. As it was
 favourable, he raised a torch. He did not return.
meditates: is thinking
list: listen, hear
several: separate
I know my hour is come: I am about to die

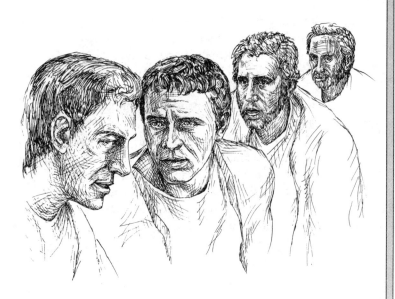

SCENE **5**

The battlefield
Enter BRUTUS, DARDANIUS, CLITUS, STRATO *and*
VOLUMNIUS

BRUTUS	Come poor remains of friends, rest on this rock.
CLITUS	Statilius showed the torch-light, but my lord,
	He came not back; he is or ta'en or slain.
BRUTUS	Sit thee down, Clitus. Slaying is the word;
	It is a deed in fashion. Hark thee, Clitus.

[*Whispers*

CLITUS	What I, my lord? No, not for all the world.
BRUTUS	Peace then, no words.
CLITUS	I'll rather kill myself.
BRUTUS	Hark thee, Dardanius.

[*Whispers*

DARDANIUS	Shall I do such a deed?
CLITUS	O Dardanius!
DARDANIUS	O Clitus!	10
CLITUS	What ill request did Brutus make to thee?
DARDANIUS	To kill him Clitus. Look, he meditates.
CLITUS	Now is that noble vessel full of grief,
	That it runs over even at his eyes.
BRUTUS	Come thither, good Volumnius, list a word.
VOLUMNIUS	What says my lord?
BRUTUS	Why this, Volumnius.
	The ghost of Cæsar hath appeared to me
	Two several times by night; at Sardis once,
	And this last night, here in Philippi fields.
	I know my hour is come.

Volumnius refuses to kill Brutus. Attack is imminent. When the others flee, Brutus asks Strato to stay.

Thou seest...goes: you can see how things are
beat us to the pit: hounded us like animals to a hole in the ground
tarry: wait
prithee: pray (beg) you
office: job
joy: rejoice
I found ... me: every man has been loyal to me
attain unto: achieve
history: story
hence: away

VOLUMNIUS	Not so, my lord. 20
BRUTUS	Nay, I am sure it is, Volumnius.
	Thou seest the world, Volumnius, how it goes;
	Our enemies have beat us to the pit.

[*Low alarums*

It is more worthy to leap in ourselves,
Than tarry till they push us. Good Volumnius,
Thou know'st that we two went to school
   together;
Even for that our love of old, I prithee
Hold thou my sword-hilts, whilst I run on it.

VOLUMNIUS   That's not an office for a friend, my lord.

[*Alarum still*

CLITUS   Fly, fly, my lord, there is no tarrying here.   30
BRUTUS   Farewell to you; and you; and you Volumnius.
Strato, thou hast been all this while asleep;
Farewell to thee too Strato. Countrymen,
My heart doth joy that yet in all my life
I found no man but he was true to me.
I shall have glory by this losing day,
More than Octavius and Mark Antony
By this vile conquest shall attain unto.
So fare you well at once, for Brutus' tongue
Hath almost ended his life's history.   40
Night hangs upon mine eyes; my bones would
   rest,
That have but laboured to attain this hour.

[*Alarum. Cry within, 'Fly, fly, fly!'*

CLITUS   Fly my lord, fly.
BRUTUS   Hence! I will follow.

[*Exeunt Clitus, Dardanius, and Volumnius*

I prithee Strato, stay thou by thy lord.

Strato helps Brutus to kill himself. Octavius and Antony arrive. The servants and friends of Brutus are spared to serve Antony and Octavius. Antony praises Brutus.

smatch: smack, touch, flavour
be still: rest
I killed ... a will: I was more reluctant to kill you
make a fire of: cremate
overcame: defeated (took his own life)
so: that is how
entertain: take into service
bestow: spend
prefer: recommend
latest: last
them all: the conspirators
save: except
that: what
in a general ... good to all: with honourable motives, believing it to be for the good of Rome
made one of them: became a conspirator
elements: qualities

	Thou art a fellow of a good respect;
	Thy life hath had some smatch of honour in it.
	Hold then my sword, and turn away thy face,
	While I do run upon it. Wilt thou Strato?
STRATO	Give me your hand first. Fare you well my lord.
BRUTUS	Farewell good Strato. [*Runs on his sword*] Cæsar,
	now be still; 50
	I killed not thee with half so good a will.

[*Dies*

Alarum. Retreat. Enter OCTAVIUS, ANTONY,
MESSALA, LUCILIUS, *and the Army*

OCTAVIUS	What man is that?
MESSALA	My master's man. Strato, where is thy master?
STRATO	Free from the bondage you are in Messala;
	The conquerors can but make a fire of him.
	For Brutus only overcame himself.
	And no man else hath honour by his death.
LUCILIUS	So Brutus should be found. I thank thee Brutus,
	That thou hast proved Lucilius' saying true.
OCTAVIUS	All that served Brutus, I will entertain them. 60
	Fellow, wilt thou bestow thy time with me?
STRATO	Ay, if Messala will prefer me to you.
OCTAVIUS	Do so, good Messala.
MESSALA	How died my master, Strato?
STRATO	I held the sword, and he did run on it.
MESSALA	Octavius, then take him to follow thee,
	That did the latest service to my master.
ANTONY	This was the noblest Roman of them all.
	All the conspirators save only he
	Did that they did in envy of great Cæsar; 70
	He only, in a general honest thought
	And common good to all, made one of them.
	His life was gentle, and the elements
	So mixed in him that Nature might stand up

Octavius pays his respects to Brutus. The battle is over.

virtue: good qualities
use: treat
ordered honourably: dressed with honour
call the field to rest: stop the fighting
part: share

ACTIVITIES

Keeping track

1 What is the difference between the Cassius we see in Act 5 scene 1, lines 78-89, and the Cassius who spoke to Casca in Act 1 scene 3?

2 The death of the standard-bearer is shocking, coming so soon after the optimistic note of Act 5 scene 2. Are you shocked that Cassius has done such a thing?

3 What does Pindarus tell Cassius about Titinius?

4 What actually happened to Titinius?

5 How does Brutus' reaction to Cassius' death differ from his reaction to his wife's death?

6 'Thou hast proved Lucilius' saying true' (Act 5 scene 5, line 59). Lucilius is referring to Act 5 scene 4, lines 24-25:
'When you do find him, or alive or dead,
He will be found like Brutus, like himself.'
What did Lucilius mean? Was Brutus 'like himself' in death?

And say to all the world 'This was a man.'

OCTAVIUS According to his virtue let us use him,
With all respect, and rites of burial.
Within my tent his bones tonight shall lie,
Most like a soldier, ordered honourably.
So call the field to rest, and let's away,   90
To part the glories of this happy day.

[*Exeunt*

Discussion

1 The parley turns into an exchange of insults and
accusations rather than an effort to make peace. But was it
really possible to avoid the battle of Philippi, knowing the
characters involved and the reasons for the dispute?
What steps do you think both sides would have had to take
for a truce to be agreed?
Was it likely that either side would give way?

2 Titinius says of Cassius, 'Alas, thou hast 'misconstrued
every thing'. In fact, how often did Cassius get things
wrong, compared with Brutus, for instance?

3 Titinius commits suicide, declaring, 'This is a Roman's
part.' Cassius and Brutus also kill themselves. In another
Shakespeare play, Macbeth is besieged by the enemy and
thinks about suicide, but then he says, 'Why should I play
the Roman fool, and die on mine own sword?' Is suicide in
these circumstances a noble or foolish act?

Drama

'The glories of this happy day'

Pair work.

After a battle, the media would be keen to get a variety of accounts from different people who were involved. Who could have been interviewed after the battle of Philippi?

1 Look closely at Act 5.
2 Choose one of the characters that survives.
3 Find out what he would have really known.
4 Think about what he might, or might not, tell the media. It is probable, of course, that some of them may be less than honest for all sorts of reasons.
5 One of you should practise what you might say as that person, whilst the other becomes his 'agent' and advises him what to say or not say.

Whole class activity.

6 Now organise a press conference in which all these people could be interviewed with their advisers (see p242 - Hotseating).

Character

1 'The last of all the Romans, fare thee well'. When he spoke of Cassius, what do you think Brutus considered the qualities necessary for a true Roman? (Your Character log on Cassius will help you here.)
2 Brutus is often thought of as the noblest Roman of them all, rather than the noblest of all the conspirators. What is the difference?
3 Close your Character logs on Brutus, Cassius and Antony.

Close study

1 'I do not cross you, but I will do so' (Act 5 scene 1). Octavius could be talking about crossing over to the

other side of the line of battle; or he could be saying that he does not want an argument at this time, but Antony had better watch out in future.

- What do we call it when 'cross' can have two meanings?
- Do you think Octavius has in mind only one of the meanings given above, or does he deliberately leave his intentions vague?
- If he is warning Antony, how do you see their relationship developing later?

2 What do you notice about the last two lines of the play? Can you suggest why this is?

Writing

Lucius Remembers

The grandchildren of Lucius love to hear his stories of the 'old days', when he was a young man and servant to Brutus. He has stories about the night the conspirators came to the house; Portia's nervousness next day; Brutus fleeing from Rome; Brutus hearing about Portia's suicide; and many more.

As Lucius, write one of the stories about your time with Brutus, as if you were actually telling it to your grandchildren by the fire on a winter's evening.

Emperor of Rome?

Brutus, Cassius or Antony might have become Emperor of Rome. None of them did, but who would have made the best leader?

Begin your writing by saying who you think would have been best. Then mention, briefly, the other two men and say why you think they are less suitable. Finally, say what qualities your choice has which would make him a good Emperor.

Quiz

Who said the following, and to whom?

1 'But for your words, they rob the Hybla bees
   And leave them honeyless'

2 'Defiance, traitors, hurl we in your teeth'

3 'If we do meet again, why, we shall smile;
   If not, why then this parting is well made'

Who said the following about whom?

4 'A peevish schoolboy, worthless of such honour,
   Joined with a masker and a reveller!'

5 'It is impossible that ever Rome
   Should breed thy fellow'

6 'His life was gentle, and the elements
   So mixed in him that nature might stand up
   And say to all the world, "This was a man!"'

Say all you can (who said it; what it means; what is referred to; what the circumstances are; any literary devices - metaphors, puns - used) about the following:

7 'This tongue had not offended so today
   If Cassius might have ruled'

8   'Keep this man safe,
   Give him all kindness. I had rather have
   Such men my friends than enemies'

9 'This day I breathed first; time is come round,
   And where I did begin, there shall I end;
   My life is run his compass'

10 'Our enemies have beat us to the pit.
   It is more worthy to leap in ourselves
   Than tarry till they push us'

Explorations

Keeping track

When you are studying a play one of the most difficult things to do is to keep track of all the ideas and information you gain as you work on it scene by scene. It is important to keep a note of what you do. Two good ways of organising your work are to keep a Scene log (see below) and a Character log (see p231).

Scene log

As you work on each scene, make a list of the basic information about it:
- when and where it takes place
- the characters in it
- what happens.

Then add any thoughts and comments you want to remember. You could use the layouts illustrated below and on the following pages - or you may prefer to make up your own.

Act / Scene	Time/ Place	Characters	Action	Comments

The plot at a glance

1i	Flavius, Marullus, the crowd	Unrest established
1ii	The feast of Lupercal	Hint at conspiracy
1iii	The storm	Conspiracy established
2i	Brutus enlisted	Conspiracy gains credibility
2ii	Cæsar and Calphurnia	Will Caesar go to the Senate?
2iii	Artemidorus	Conspiracy not secret
2iv	Portia and Lucius	Portia aware of conspiracy
3i	Death of Cæsar	Conspiracy successful
3ii	Funeral of Cæsar	People of Rome react
3iii	Cinna the poet	Crowd out of control
4i	Antony, Octavius, Lepidus organise purge	Retribution begins
4ii	Brutus and Cassius meet	Conspirators at odds
4iii	Brutus and Cassius argue	Conspirators reconciled
5i	The parley	Chance to avoid war
5ii	Brutus orders attack	Battle begins
5iii	Cassius defeated	Cassius dies
5iv	Brutus under attack	Lucilius captured
5v	Brutus defeated	Brutus dies

The two tribunes, supporters of Pompey, show their opposition to Cæsar in their attitude to the crowd. Attending the feast, Cæsar ignores a warning. There is unrest in Rome. Cassius 'sounds out' Brutus. Casca commits himself to the conspiracy.

Brutus joins the conspiracy and is accepted as leader. In spite of Calphurnia's wishes, Cæsar is persuaded by Decius to go to the Senate House. Artemidorus has a warning for Cæsar.
Portia is worried about Brutus. The soothsayer increases her fears.

Cæsar is killed. Antony seems to support the conspirators. He forecasts civil war. Brutus' speech is well received by the crowd. Antony stirs them to revolt. Brutus and Cassius flee. The crowd run wild and kill Cinna, the poet.

The triumvirate draw up a 'hit-list'. They prepare to meet Brutus and Cassius in battle.
Cassius shows his annoyance at Brutus' treatment of him. The argument is furious, followed by reconciliation. Portia's suicide is announced. They prepare for battle. Angry insults are exchanged at the parley before the battle of Philippi. Brutus unwisely orders the attack.

Brutus defeats Octavius; Cassius, overrun by Antony, is told Titinius has been taken and he commits suicide. Lucilius, pretending to be Brutus, is captured. Antony is impressed by Lucilius' actions. Brutus, facing defeat, commits suicide. His followers join Antony and Octavius.

Character activities

Quotations

When talking or writing about a character, it is important to
be able to back up what you say by referring to the play. You
could say, 'I know this is true of this character because in
Act 1 scene 2 he says this, or does that!' You should have lots
of information for the main characters in your Character logs.
It is useful to have some of it in your head. A good way of
remembering is to have a 'nutshell' quotation for each
character - a few words which really sum up the character, or
describe him/her 'in a nutshell'. For instance, Cassius calls
Antony 'a shrewd contriver'. It would be difficult to find a
more fitting description.

Group work

Discuss some descriptions of the other main characters and
decide on 'nutshell' quotations for them.

Character logs

It is better to keep track of the characters as you are going
through the play, rather than have to go back to begin a
search for information to help you to answer a particular
question.

Character logs will help you to do this. They contain:

- key points about the character
- your reasons for choosing these
- the numbers of important lines
- short quotations to back up key points.

You will need a Character log for each main character. Your
Character log might look like the one on the next page.

Character Log

Character: Brutus

Act/ scene	Key points	Reasons	Key lines	Short quotations
1/2	Is not fooled	Asks Classius what he really wants	63–65	Into what dangers would you lead me?
	Is troubled	He loves Cæsar but fears his ambition	82	

Character

Weighing up characters

Who do the qualities on each of the scales below belong to?
Note: not all the characteristics are included, just enough to
help you recognise them; nor are the characteristics in order
of importance.

You can use the information below as a starting point for
drawing together the characteristics of the most important
people in the play for future use in written and spoken work.
If you have the characteristics divided into positive (good) and
negative (bad) qualities you are well on the way to being
prepared to tackle a Character essay (see p 249). You will
need to keep your Character logs for reference and
quotations.

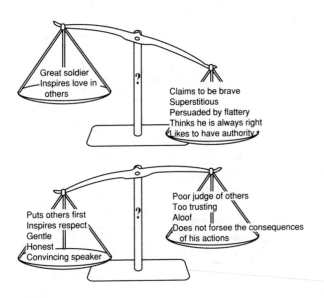

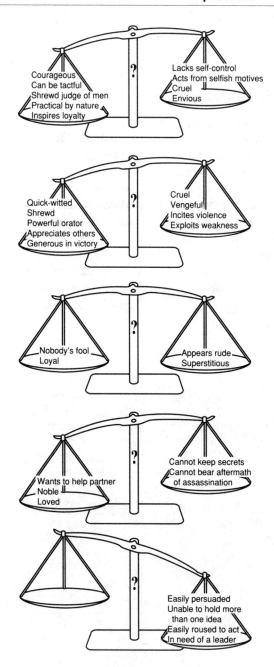

Themes

People and power 1

Throughout history people have been concerned with the question: what makes good government? There are broadly three types of system which have been used:
- dictatorship (government by one person)
- oligarchy (government by a select group)
- democracy (government by an elected body).

No-one claims that any one of these systems is perfect: there are arguments for and against each one of them.

Below are given some of the arguments for (pros) and some of the arguments against (cons) these three forms of government. Can you think of other points to add to each list?

	Pros	Cons
Dictatorship	1 Decisions made quickly 2 Few surprise decisions	1 Public opinion ignored 2 Many selfish decisions
Oligarchy	1 Decisions fairly quick 2 More opinions taken	1 Will benefit only a few 2 Public still ignored
Democracy	1 Responsible to voters 2 Regular elections	1 Decision-making slow 2 Fear of public opinion

Which of the systems above seems to you to be the best form of government? Are you any closer to deciding what makes good government?

People and power 2

An argument between the ghosts of Cæsar and Pompey about power might have consisted of the following points:

I believed in the Senate.	But the Senate was made up of the well-off. What about the common man?
I distrusted one-man rule.	The Senate was weak. The people needed leadership.
But you were always seeking personal glory.	If you mean by defeating the enemies of Rome, then I was guilty.
What was to stop you becoming a tyrant?	The people. When they petitioned me, I listened.
But you named an heir. That was the behaviour of a king.	I felt that there had to be continuity.

For each of Cæsar's replies, Pompey could have made further comment. What might he have said?

Loyalty and Friendship

Loyalty and friendship are both important in *Julius Cæsar*.
Indeed, it is Antony's loyalty to, and friendship for, Cæsar
which bring about the conspirators' downfall.

It is interesting to look closely at Brutus and Cassius; their
relationship to each other and to other people. There are two
things to think about: A who inspired friendship, and who
inspired loyalty?

B were Brutus and Cassius close friends?

To help with question A, first look at the details below.

Friendship, n. – closeness of people sharing love and respect
Loyalty, n. – behaviour showing faithfulness to duty

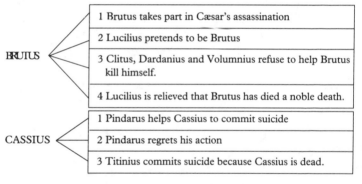

BRUTUS
1 Brutus takes part in Cæsar's assassination
2 Lucilius pretends to be Brutus
3 Clitus, Dardanius and Volumnius refuse to help Brutus kill himself.
4 Lucilius is relieved that Brutus has died a noble death.

CASSIUS
1 Pindarus helps Cassius to commit suicide
2 Pindarus regrets his action
3 Titinius commits suicide because Cassius is dead.

How would you fill the gaps in this table? (Tip: think about
Brutus 2 and Brutus 4 at the same time)

EVENT	LOYALTY/FRIENDSHIP
BRUTUS 1	LOYALTY to the people overcomes friendship for Cæsar
BRUTUS 2	
BRUTUS 3	
BRUTUS 4	
CASSIUS 1	LOYALTY of a slave to his master
CASSIUS 2	
CASSIUS 3	

Before deciding on an answer to question B, look again at
how Brutus and Cassius say farewell to each other in Act 4
scene 3, line 237.

Honour

Can you say what the missing words are?

1 'Set _____ in one eye and death i' th'other.
   And I will look on both indifferently.'

2 'For let the gods so speed me as I love
   The name of _____ more than I fear death.'
                              'and no man here

3 'Believe me for mine _____ , and have respect to
   mine _____ , that you may believe.'

4 'But Brutus says he was ambitious,
   And Brutus is an _____ man.'

Not surprisingly, these words are spoken by, or about, Brutus.

Find short quotations of your own to illustrate the same
theme in each of the circumstances listed below.
   i   Brutus' reasons for refusing to take an oath (Act 2 scene 1);
   ii Brutus' reason for not killing Antony (Act 2 scene 1);
   iii Brutus' reaction to being captured (Act 5 scene 1);
   iv Cassius' intention to kill himself rather than to be ordered
       around by Cæsar (Act 1 scene 2, Act 1 scene 3).

'I have a man's mind but a woman's might' – the role of women

In Rome's male-dominated society Calphurnia and Portia are
minor figures. In groups re-read Act 2, scenes 1, 2 and 4.
Discuss the following questions.
- Are Calphurnia and Portia wimps or are they hampered by
  the role women have to play in their society?
- How do you think Shakespeare views Calphurnia and Portia?
- Would women today act differently when trying to
  persuade their partners to do something? (e.g. when
  Calphurnia tries to persuade Cæsar not to go to the
  Senate-House).

Shakespeare's language

It is easy to look at the text of this play and say to yourself, 'I'm never going to understand that!' But it is important not to be put off. Remember that there are two reasons why Shakespeare's language may seem strange at first:

1 He was writing four hundred years ago and the English language has changed over the centuries.
2 He wrote mainly in verse. As a result he sometimes changed the order of words to make them fit the verse form, and he used a large number of 'tricks of the trade': figures of speech and other verse techniques.

On page 240 you will find advice on tackling the 'difficult bits'.

Language change

This can cause three main kinds of problem:

Grammar

Since the end of the 16th century, there have been some changes in English grammar. Some examples:

1 Thee, thou, thy, and the verb forms that go with them:
   And then I swore *thee*, saving of *thy* life,
   That whatsoever I did bid *thee* do,
   Thou shouldst attempt it. Come now, keep *thine* oath.
2 Words contract (shorten) in different ways. For example:
   'tis rather than *it's*
   who is't for *who is it*
3 Some of the 'little words' are different. For example:
   an for *if*

Words that have changed their meaning

Sometimes you will come across words that you think you know, but discover that they don't mean what you expect them to mean. For example:
presently (Act 3 scene 1 line 142) meant *at once* in Shakespeare's day. Now it means *in a while*.
Nowadays *lover* refers to someone with whom the speaker is in love. In this play, however, *lover* means *friend*.

Words that have gone out of use

These are the most obvious and most frequent causes of difficulty. Shakespeare had - and used - a huge vocabulary. He loved using words, and pushing them to their limits. So you will come across many words you have not met before. They are usually explained in the notes. But before rushing to look up every single word, look at the advice on page 240.

The language of the play

Most of *Julius Cæsar* is in *blank verse*, but parts are in *prose* and some sections are in *rhymed verse*.

Blank verse

The main part of the play is written in lines of ten syllables, with a repeated even pattern of weak and strong 'beats':
*You **blocks**, you **stones**, you **worse** than **sense**less **things**!*
(ti **tum** ti **tum** ti **tum** ti **tum** ti **tum**)
If Shakespeare had made every line exactly the same, the play would soon become very monotonous, so he varies the rhythm in a number of ways. Often he just changes the pattern of weak and strong slightly:
***Have** you not **made** an **uni**versal **shout**?*
(**tum** ti ti **tum** ti **tum tum** ti ti **tum**)

He also writes so that sentences sometimes finish at the end of a line, and at other times in the middle:

>   *Cassius,*
> *Be not deceived. If I have veiled my look,*
> *I turn the trouble of my countenance*
> *Merely upon myself.*

So the verse of the play has a strong but varied rhythm. Most of the lines do not rhyme, so they are 'blank' - hence the term *blank verse*.

Rhymed verse

Sometimes Shakespeare uses a pattern of rhymed lines. It may be just two successive lines (a *rhyming couplet*), often rounding off a scene:

> *So call the field to rest, and let's away,*
> *To part the glories of this happy day.*

Prose

In some scenes, characters' speeches are not written in blank or rhymed verse, but in 'ordinary sentences' - prose. If you look at the play as a whole, you will see that prose is used for certain characters and situations. Look, for example, at these sections:

Act 1 scene 1 lines 1-36; Act 4 scene 3 (most of the scene). Can you work out what those characters and situations are?

Working out the difficult bits

If you come across a section of the play that you find difficult to understand, try any or all of these approaches:

1   Read the whole section through and try to get an idea of the gist of it - roughly what it is about.
2   Try to pin down which particular sentences are causing the problem.
3   Work out the pattern of the whole sentence - look to see if Shakespeare has changed the ordinary word order to fit the verse.

4 Try reading the sentence aloud a few times.
5 Don't feel that you have to understand every word in the play - very few people do!
6 Don't feel that you've got to read every note and explanation in this book - use them when you really need them.

Drama activities

Most of these activities can be done in small groups or by the class as a whole. They work by slowing down the action of the play and helping you focus on a small section of it - so that you can think more deeply about characters, plot and themes.

Hotseating

Hotseating means putting one of the characters 'under the microscope' at a particular point in the play. This is how it works:

1 Begin by choosing a particular character and a particular moment in the play. For example you might choose Cassius at the moment when he invites Brutus to kill him (Act 4 scene 3).
2 One person (student or teacher) is selected to be the chosen character.
3 That person sits 'in the hotseat', with the rest of the group arranged round in a semi-circle, or a circle.
4 The rest then ask questions about how the character feels, why s/he has acted in that way, and so on. Try to keep the questions going and not to give the person in the hotseat too much time to think.

Variations

1 The questioners themselves take on roles. (In the example above they could be Brutus' men.)
2 Characters can be hotseated at a series of key moments in a scene to see how their opinions and attitudes change.
3 The questioners can take different attitudes to the character, for example:
    ● aggressive
    ● pleading
    ● disbelieving.

Freeze!

It is very useful to be able to 'stop the action' and concentrate on a single moment in the play. You can do this in a number of ways.

Photographs

Imagine that someone has taken a photograph of a particular moment, or that - as if it were a film or video - the action has been frozen. Once you have chosen the moment, you can work in a number of different ways:

- Act that part of the scene and then 'Freeze!' - you will probably find it easier if you have a 'director' standing outside the scene to shout 'Freeze!'
- Discuss what the photograph should look like and then arrange yourselves into the photograph.
- One at a time place yourselves in the photograph; each person 'entering' it must take notice of what is there already.
- Once you have arranged the photograph, take it in turns to come out of it and comment on it, with suggestions for improvements.

There are a number of ways in which you can develop your photograph:

- Each person takes it in turn to speak his/her thoughts at that moment in the scene.
- The photograph is given a caption.
- Some members of the group do not take part in the photograph. Instead they provide a sound track of speech or sound effects, or both.

Statues

Make a statue like this:
1 Select a moment in the play, or a title from the play (e.g. 'Honourable men').
2 Choose one member of the group to be the sculptor. That person then arranges the rest of the group, one at a time to

make the statue. Statues are different from photographs in two important ways:

- they are made by a 'sculptor' and tell us about the sculptor's view of the person or event;
- if they talk, they tell us about what they can 'see'. For example if there was a statue of the assassination of Cæsar, placed in the streets of Rome, it could only 'tell' us about how the citizens of Rome behaved when they saw it. (If you want the conspirators to speak their thoughts at that moment, then hotseat them, or make a photograph.)

Forum theatre

In Forum theatre, one or two people take on roles and the rest of the group are 'directors'. It works like this:

1 Select a moment in the play. (For example the moment when Antony sees Cæsar's body for the first time.)
2 Select a member of the group to be Antony.
3 Organise your working area, so that everyone knows where the other characters are, where characters make entrances and exits, and so on.
4 Begin by asking Antony to offer his own first thoughts about position, gesture, and movement.
5 The directors then experiment with different ways of presenting that moment. They can:
   - ask Antony to take up a particular position, use a particular gesture, move in a certain way;
   - ask him to speak in a particular way;
   - discuss with Antony how he might move or speak and why - for example to communicate a certain set of thoughts and feelings.
6 The short sequence can be repeated a number of times, until the directors have used up all their ideas about their interpretation.

Talk it over: ideas for discussion

These discussions will be most effective if held with groups of three or four. When you have had time to exchange ideas and come to some conclusions, share your thoughts with others in the class. Sometimes this 'reporting back' will involve the whole class, sometimes it will mean comparing notes with one other group. On occasions, the original groups can be split and new groupings made, with each member bringing the thoughts and suggestions from their first group.

1 In Act 4 scene 1 we see the triumvirate compiling a blacklist of enemies to be killed. In Act 4 scene 2 we learn that Brutus treated his enemies kindly in the belief that he could win them over. Which approach is more sensible, do you think? Is there another way of dealing with enemies which is better?

2 The confrontation with Cæsar's ghost seems to have little effect on Brutus in Act 4 scene 3. What later events seem to indicate that the ghost has indeed made an impact on him? In what way has it changed him?

3 In Act 5 scene 1 Octavius accuses the conspirators of being traitors. Brutus denies this. What would Brutus' argument be when explaining his point of view?

4 In Act 5 scene 2 Brutus seems unusually agitated, and he gives a command for the battle to start which proves to be a serious error. Can you think of reasons for his state of mind?

5 On Cassius' death, Titinius predicts the end of the Republic, the end of life as they know it: 'The sun of Rome is set. Our day is gone.' In today's world, what does it mean to people if their lives are turned upside down by war or natural disasters? What would it mean to you if such a thing happened? How would your life be different? What would you have to do without? What would you miss most?

6 Brutus' death brings an end to this part of the history of the Roman Empire, and to this play. It is a time for looking back and asking, 'What if...?' For instance, we might ask:
- what if Cæsar had listened to Calphurnia?
- what if Brutus had refused to join the conspirators?
- what if the assassination had not taken place?
- what if Antony had been killed with Cæsar?
- what if Brutus had spoken after Antony at the funeral?
- what if Brutus had not given the wrong orders to the army?
- what if Cassius had not committed suicide?

However, it might be said that all these things were bound to happen, given the characters involved. What do you think? Give your reasons.

7 Imagine that Casca is looking over your shoulder at this moment. He has seen events unfolding. He sighs and says, 'And they laughed at me, didn't they?' To what would he be referring? How could he argue in detail that what he reported has now taken place?

8 How important are the citizens of Rome to:
Flavius and Marullus; Brutus; the conspirators; Antony; the outcome of the play?

9 Think of some of the features of the play which would be difficult to 'stage' convincingly: battle scenes, armies, Cæsar's ghost, for instance. Which would be most difficult? How would you overcome the difficulties?

10 Decide whether *Julius Cæsar* would make a good school play. You will have to take into account the action and the language, of course, and do not forget the nature of the audience. You will also have to consider some of the difficulties of putting this play on stage. (Listed in Question 9.)

Writing activities

These activities allow you to respond imaginatively to the play .

Imaginative Writing

1 Lepidus - His Story

We do not know much at all about Lepidus (see
Introduction and Act 4 scene 1). He was by no means
insignificant because he was a triumvir for 7 years. Create a
biography of Lepidus, based on the little we do know.

2 Cassius' Thoughts

Before Brutus and Cassius meet in Act 4 scene 2 Cassius
has much on his mind. Brutus has ignored a letter which
Cassius sent on behalf of one of his men whom Brutus had
accused of doing wrong. We know that Cassius believes
that Brutus has his faults, too. No doubt Cassius would
rehearse in his mind what he would say when they met. As
Cassius write down the thoughts that go through your head
when you know you are going to meet Brutus; thoughts
that will eventually cause you to greet Brutus with the
aggressive, 'You have done me wrong.'

3 Come Antony, Away!

After the parley, Octavius and Antony withdraw with their
armies. They have both reacted angrily to Brutus' and
Cassius' remarks, and so have a great deal to say to each
other: about the situation; about Cassius and Brutus and
their attitude; about particular accusations that have been
made; about things that have been hinted at; and about the
assassination of Cæsar, perhaps. In script form, write the
conversation between Antony and Octavius.

Writing about the play: giving an opinion

Much of the writing you have done so far, in the Activities sections of this book, and in English lessons in the past, has probably been personal (based on your own experiences), or creative (telling stories which you have made up), or descriptive (describing scenes or events).

In the Activities sections at the end of Acts 3, 4 and 5 you are also asked to tackle a different kind of writing - writing in which you are asked to make a judgement about characters or events in the play.

Writing of this kind is roughly similar to a mathematical problem, but the good part about it is that there is no 'right' answer. Your opinion, if you can show your 'working out', is as good as anyone else's.

This is how a sum works:	*This is how your writing works:*	
	Introduction: what you are writing about	
35	The first point you want to make	+
+		
46	The second point you want to make	+
+		
21	The third point you want to make	+
+		
14	The fourth point you want to make	=
―――		
Answer	Conclusion: your 'answer' to the question	

The questions on the opposite page give you an opportunity to practise this type of lay-out. See also **Writing about character** (p250) .

1 **Loyalty and friendship**
   In Julius Cæsar we see example of men risking everything for
   the love of others: Brutus joins the conspiracy for the sake of
   the Roman people; Antony bravely approaches the conspirators
   after Cæsar's death because of his regard for Cæsar; and
   Lucilius is prepared to die to protect Brutus. In the case of
   Titinius, he actually commits suicide for his love of Cassius.
   Choose one of these examples, or another which you might
   think more suitable, and write about it in detail, explaining:
   what it tells us about the people involved; and why you think it
   is a good example of loyalty and/or friendship.

2 **Honour at stake**
   You have already looked at the disagreement between Cassius
   and Brutus in Act 4 scene 3, and what it shows us about the
   differences in character (page 190).
   Some people have said that the argument is really about
   honour; about reputation. Do you agree? Is it important that
   each man should respect the other? Is the reconciliation vital to
   them as individuals, as well as to the Republican cause?
   Write about the disagreement saying how far honour is
   involved.

3 **Calphurnia's role**
   'Calphurnia only appears in Act 2 scene 2 so that we can see
   how clever Decius Brutus is.'
   Do you understand what this means? Do you agree with the
   critic who said it? Is Calphurnia really so insignificant? (It is true
   that Cæsar talks about his wife's dream, not Calphurnia
   herself?)
   Write about how you interpret Calphurnia's role in this scene.

4 **'Julius Cæsar'**
   Would you recommend this play to friends, or not?
   Begin by saying how you felt when you knew you were going to
   study a Shakespeare play; end by saying how you feel about
   Julius Cæsar now. In the 'body' of your essay you will write
   about the things which led you to your conclusion, some of
   which might be: character, plot, themes, historical background,
   language, theatrical technique and relevance to modern life.

Writing about character

Sometimes you will be asked to do a piece of writing which is based on one character. Just as in **Writing about the play: giving an opinion**, p248 there are three points to remember:

1 The introduction makes clear to the reader that you have understood the title.
2 The 'body' of your writing leads the reader from one point to the next.
3 The conclusion is an 'answer' to the title, arrived at by weighing up the points you have made in (2).

In the case of character writing you will need full character notes to work from. Organise your notes according to the title of the work.

If you are given the title 'Mark Antony', you might follow this outline:	If the title is a question such as 'Would you trust Mark Antony?' you have to decide on your answer before you begin to write, and work towards that answer. Let us assume that you think the answer to the question is 'Yes'.
1 Introduction: Say who Mark Antony is.	1 Introduction: e.g. Antony is a many-sided character.
2 His second most important characteristic.	2 Characteristics making him untrustworthy.
3 His minor characteristics.	3 His 'trustworthy' characteristics.
4 His most important characteristic.	
5 Conclusion: what sort of man he is.	4 Conclusion: an 'answer' to the question.

Practice questions

1 **'This Was A Man'**
Although circumstances made them enemies, Antony says
of Brutus: 'His life was gentle, and the elements
> So mixed in him that Nature might stand up
> And say to all the world 'This was a man'
We know that Brutus has weaknesses, but what is it about
him which causes everybody who knows him to regard him
with the greatest respect?

2 **'If Cæsar had stabbed their mothers . . .'**
Cæsar is loved, indeed idolised, by the people of Rome.
Casca says that they are ready to forgive Cæsar for any
weakness: 'If Cæsar had stabbed their mothers, they would
have done no less.'
In the play, what qualities do we see in Cæsar which made
this adoration understandable? On the other hand, does he
have characteristics which make it unlikely that anyone
would look up to him?
On balance, do you think Cæsar deserves the respect and
affection of his people?

3 **Mark Antony**
Antony is variously described as 'a shrewd contriver'. 'but a
limb of Cæsar', 'a masker and a reveller' and 'the noble
Antony'. An opinion about him seems to depend very
much on who is speaking and what the circumstances are.
You have followed Antony throughout the play. What sort
of man do you think he is?

4 **'A Woman Well- Reputed'**
It has been said that Portia does not appear after Act 2
because she is drawing too much attention to herself, and
away from the main plot. Can this be true? Is she such an
interesting woman?
Look closely at Portia's characteristics and decide whether
you find her interesting or not.

Short questions

Sometimes you may be asked to write a short response to a question or topic. The topics below call for short pieces of writing (two paragraphs at the most). In each case you will need to pay detailed attention to a particular part of the play.

1 **Act 1 scene 1**
At the end of this first scene, what have you learned about Julius Cæsar and his standing in the eyes of his contemporaries? How has Shakespeare achieved this?

2 **Act 1 scene 2 and Act 1 scene 3**
Some of your impressions from the first scene are reinforced in scenes 2 and 3. How is this done through the different characters?

3 **Act 2 scene 1**
How does the behaviour of Caius Ligarius sum up what others have had to say about Brutus?

4 **Act 2 scene 2**
Is there anything about Cæsar's behaviour at the end of this scene which might cause you to remember the crowd's attitude to him in the first scene of the play?

5 **Act 3 scene 1**
The crowd fled after the murder of Cæsar. Sum up their reasons for doing so.

6 **Act 3 scene 2**
How does Antony differ from Marullus (Act 1 scene 1) in his attitude to the crowd? Is there a reason for this? How does Antony show that Flavius was accurate in his judgement of the crowd?

7 **Act 4 scene 3**
Bearing in mind what you have seen of Portia earlier in the play, do you find her suicide believable?

8 **Act 5 scene 5**
After his death Brutus is praised by Antony and Octavius. Do they mean what they say? If they had come across Cassius' body, would they have spoken about him in the same way?

Glossary

Alarum: A call to arms, often a trumpet call.

Alliteration: A figure of speech in which a number of words close to each other in a piece of writing begin with the same sound:

Fierce fiery warriors fight upon the clouds

Alliteration helps to draw attention to these words.

Anachronism: In a historical drama the writer may accidentally or deliberately allow characters to refer to things from a later period, which they would not have known about. This is called 'anachronism':

BRUTUS: Peace, count the clock.

CASSIUS: The clock hath stricken three.

Clocks had not been invented in Cæsar's time.

Antithesis: A figure of speech in which the writer brings two opposite or contrasting ideas up against each other:

Cowards die many times before their deaths,
The valiant never taste of death but once.

Apostrophe: When a character suddenly speaks directly to someone or something, which may or may not be present:

O, pardon me thou bleeding piece of earth

Blank verse: See page 239

Dramatic irony: A situation in a play when the audience (and possibly some of the characters) know something that one or more of the characters don't. In a pantomime, for example, young children will often shout to tell the hero that a dreadful monster is creeping up behind him, unseen. An example from *Julius Cæsar* is when Calphurnia fails to persuade Cæsar to stay at home, when we know that the conspiracy depends on his going to the Capitol.

Exeunt: A Latin word meaning 'They go away', used for the departure of characters from a scene.

Exit: A Latin word meaning 'He (or she) goes away', used for the departure of a character from a scene.

Hyperbole: Deliberate exaggeration, for dramatic effect.
Are you not moved when all the sway of the earth
Shakes like a thing infirm?

Irony: When someone says one thing and means another,
often to make fun of, tease, or satirise someone else:
For Brutus is an honourable man,
So are they all, all honourable men.
See also **Dramatic irony**

Metaphor: A figure of speech in which one person, or thing,
or idea is described as if it were another.
CASSIUS: *And why should Cæsar be a tyrant then?*
Poor man, I know he would not be a wolf
But that he sees the Romans are but sheep;
He were no lion, were not Romans hinds.

Onomatopoeia: Using words that are chosen because they
mimic the sound of what is being described:
Horses did neigh and dying men did groan,
And ghosts did shriek and squeal about the streets.

Personification: Referring to a thing or an idea as if it were a
person:
O murd'rous slumber
Layest thou thy leaden mace upon my boy,
That plays thee music?

Play on words: see Pun

Pun: A figure of speech in which the writer uses a word that
has more than one meaning. Both meanings of the word
are used to make a joke. In Act 1 scene 1, the cobbler has
already made a pun on the word 'soles' ('souls') when he
says, 'I meddle with no tradesman's matters, not women's
matters, but with all.' The play is on the word 'all', an 'awl'
being a cobbler's tool.
Sometimes a pun may be used to make a more serious
point. Cassius complains of Cæsar's overbearing self-
importance:
Now is it Rome indeed, and room enough,
When there is in it but one man.

Simile: A comparison between two things which the writer

makes clear by using words such as 'like' or 'as':
Why man, he doth bestride the world like a Colossus

Soliloquy: When a character is alone on stage, or separated from the other characters in some way and speaks apparently to himself or herself.